D0839068

C I T Y P A C K
Miami

By Mick Sinclair

2ND EDITION

Fodor's Travel Publications
New York • Toronto • London • Sydney • Auckland

W W W . F O D O R S . C O M

Contents

About this book

KEY TO SYMBOLS

✚	Map reference to the location on the fold-out map accompanying this book	🚢	Nearest riverboat or ferry stop
✉	Address	♿	Facilities for visitors with disabilities
☎	Telephone number	✋	Admission charge
🕐	Opening/closing times	↔	Other nearby places of interest
🍴	Restaurant or café on premises or nearby	❓	Tours, lectures, or special events
🚇	Nearest Metro train station	➤	Indicates the page where you will find a fuller description
🚌	Nearest bus route	ℹ	Tourist information

Citypack Miami is divided into six sections to cover the six most important aspects of your visit to Miami. It includes:

- The city and its people
- Itineraries, walks, and excursions
- The top 25 sights to visit
- What makes the city special
- Restaurants, hotels, stores, and nightlife
- Practical information

In addition, easy-to-read side panels provide extra facts and snippets, highlights of places to visit, and invaluable practical advice.

CROSS-REFERENCES

To help you make the most of your visit, cross-references, indicated by ➤, show you where to find additional information about a place or subject.

MAPS

The fold-out map in the wallet at the back of the book is a comprehensive street plan of Miami. All the map references given in the book refer to this map. For example, the Bass Museum of Art on Park Avenue has the following information: ✚ M5—indicating the grid square of the map in which the Bass Museum of Art will be found.

The downtown maps found on the inside front and back covers of the book itself are for quick reference. They show the top 25 sights, described on pages 24–48, which are clearly plotted by number (**1**– **25**, not page number) from west to east.

ADMISSION CHARGES

An indication of the admission charge (for all attractions) is given by categorizing the standard adult rate as follows:

✋ expensive (over $13), moderate ($7–13), inexpensive (under $7).

MIAMI
life

INTRODUCING MIAMI

Miami defined

Formally, the city of Miami comprises only Downtown and its immediate vicinity—a fraction of what is generally regarded as Miami. The greater Miami area, the city as the world thinks of it, includes 27 municipalities, among them far-flung suburban areas such as South Miami and Hialeah, and self-governing cities-within-the-city such as Miami Beach, Coral Gables, and Coconut Grove.

When salsa rhythms merge with a warm ocean breeze whispering through the palm fronds and the sun gleams on pastel walls of the art-deco buildings, there is only one place you can be: Miami. A sleepy retirement and vacation city in the 1970s and the butt of many a joke, Miami is now a vibrant multinational metropolis.

Throughout the 1980s, Miami exploited its potential at the geographical heart of the Americas and emerged as the economic hub of U.S.–Latin American trade, providing a safe haven for billions of South and Central American dollars from countries whose economies faced rocketing inflation and social turmoil. Simultaneously, the hundreds of art-deco buildings in the then unfashionable southern end of Miami Beach—the area known as South Beach—were discovered languishing in disrepair. Later painted and restored, the structures provided a scintillating background for the groundbreaking cop show *Miami Vice* in the 1980s, and for a major Calvin Klein advertising campaign that projected the South Beach look around the world.

Now studded with recording studios, model agencies, trendy cafés, wonderful restaurants, and celebrity-owned nightclubs, South Beach *is* Miami for many visitors who happily get no further. It has the pick of the city's hotels and is easy to get around on foot. A gorgeous beach frames its art-deco buildings, and, for those whose energy is unlimited, the bars and discos are often still

Above: Art deco on Ocean Drive—the Cardozo hotel
Right: Miami Beach

going strong at 5AM. Yet while South Beach is the focal point, areas such as Coral Gables, Coconut Grove, and Key Biscayne also have much to recommend them.

Curiously, if a single element underpins modern Miami, it is one over which the city had absolutely no control: the Cuban revolution. When Fidel Castro took power in 1959, it was the start of an exodus that during the late 1960s saw a Cuban arriving in Miami every seven minutes. The present population of Cubans, including Miami-born Cubans, numbers 600,000. Cuban food, Cuban music, and Cuban passion for life shapes the contemporary city, be it through local politics—Miami elected its first Cuban-American mayor in 1985—or the fact that wherever you go, you are never far from an invigorating shot of *café Cubano*.

Making Los Angeles look like the Old World, and cradles of American history such as New York

Miami "Spanglish"

Given that half of Miami's residents have Spanish as a mother tongue, it should be no surprise to hear Spanish being spoken widely, or to find it more commonly heard than English in many parts of the city. A greater surprise to the ear is "Spanglish," an only-in-Miami mix of English and Cuban Spanish most likely to be heard spoken between Miami-Cubans as they effortlessly mix the two languages in the same sentence.

Miami Beach tanning

Miami heat

It is easy to underestimate the strength of the Miami sun. The city sizzles year-round and anyone not sensibly protected risks severe sunburn. So use a sunscreen, and if you burn easily, use the strongest you can find. To avoid the sun at its most powerful, limit time spent outdoors between 11AM and 2PM, wear a hat and sunglasses, and imbibe plenty of (nonalcoholic) liquid.

and Boston seem like ancient civilizations, Miami was labeled "the city of the future" in the 1980s, but the tag could have been applied at almost any time in its past. Little more than 100 years ago, Miami was a mosquito-tormented outpost (accessible only by boat) with a population of a few hundred living in wooden shacks. Miami grew into the nation's favorite 1950s vacation spot, and today, while Cubans and Anglo-Americans make up the bulk of its population, it is remarkably multiethnic, its residents drawn from every part of South and Central America and across the Caribbean. Some 100,000 Haitans call Miami home, alongwith immigrants from China, Greece, Israel, Italy, Russia, and Sweden.

Although inequalities of wealth and opportunity have seen parts of the city erupt into violence on several occasions, the greatest catastrophe of recent years was a natural one. In August 1992, Hurricane Andrew affected every Miamian, regardless of ethnic origin or income. Afterward, rebuilding the city forged a spirit of together-ness perhaps not seen since the pioneer days of a century ago.

In 1999, a legacy of the Cuban revolution had a similarly large—but much more divisive—impact on the city. The rescue by a Miami-Cuban fisherman of five-year-old Elian Gonzalez, who had fled by raft from Cuba with his mother, triggered worldwide media interest and split Miami in two. Most Miami Cubans believed the boy should stay with his relatives in Miami rather than be returned to the hated Castro regime. Many others in the city wanted the boy reunited with his father in Cuba. The affair, which concluded with Elian's return to Cuba, served to remind the world of Miami's large and vocal Cuban population and its influ-ential role in U.S.–Cuba relations.

MIAMI IN FIGURES

General Information
- Miles from Orlando: 228.
- Miles from New York: 1,091.
- Miles from San Francisco: 3,510.
- Miles from Havana: 230.
- Miles from London: 4,400.
- Miles from Berlin: 5,026.

Geography
- Latitude: N 25° 46 minutes.
- Longitude: W 80° 12 minutes.

Population
- Greater Miami area: 2 million.
- City of Miami: 360,000.
- Coconut Grove: 18,000.
- Coral Gables: 41,406.
- Miami Beach: 93,000.
- Key Biscayne: 19,000.

Multinational Origins
- Cubans: 770,000.
- Haitians: 100,000.
- Puerto Ricans: 72,000.
- Jamaicans & Bahamians: 40,000.
- Dominicans: 23,000.
- Miami residents speaking Spanish at home: 50 percent.

Domestic Visitors
- Annual domestic visitors: 4.4 million.

International Visitors
- Annual international visitors: 5.4 million.
- From South America: 39.4 percent.
- From Europe: 25.6 percent.
- From Caribbean: 13.6 percent.

Weather
- Average daily temperature: 75°F.
- Hottest month: August, average daytime high 89°F.
- Coolest month: January, average daytime low 59°F.
- Wettest month: June, 9.3 inches.
- Driest month: December, 1.8 inches.

Getting Around
- Miami International Airport: 33.5 million annual passengers, second busiest in U.S.
- Port of Miami: 3 million annual passengers, busiest passenger port in the world.
- Taxi cabs: 1,827.
- Bus routes: 70.

9

A CHRONOLOGY

1513 Spaniard Juan Ponce de León makes the first European landing in what becomes Florida. His continuing navigation of the coast includes a landing at the future site of Miami.

1821 After possession of Florida has switched between the Spanish and the British, it becomes a U.S. possession. U.S. citizens settle predominantly in the north of the state; in three subsequent Seminole Wars, the Seminole people are driven into the swamplands of the Everglades.

1843 Parcels of land in Miami, a riverside hamlet, are sold for $1 each. The name "Miami" is allegedly derived from a Tequesta (the name given to a native tribe of the area) word meaning "sweet water."

1847 Miami's first trading post is built on the banks of the Miami River.

1860 Miami's population is 60. No roads reach the settlement, which can be accessed only by boat.

1874 The opening of its post office ensures Miami is added to official maps.

1880s Coconut Grove, a settlement several miles from Miami, now engulfed by the city, increases in size and renown with the arrival of the Peacock family, whose hotel becomes the area's first lodging and who bring a population of Bahamians to work for them. Within 10 years, Coconut Grove is described as southern Florida's "largest and most influential" community.

1896 Standard Oil tycoon Henry Flagler extends his railroad south to Miami and opens a hotel on the river, bringing increased settlement. The same year, its population numbering 300, Miami officially becomes a city.

1900 Miami's population reaches 5,000.

1913 Entrepreneur Carl Fisher begins the dredging

operation that creates a beach for Miami Beach. Tourists from the northeast flock to it.

1921 Developer George Merrick sells the first plot of Coral Gables. A land-buying frenzy grips Miami.

1926 The monetary muddle caused by the land boom and by the realization that many purchasers have bought worthless plots, causes banks to collapse and brings a severe slump. A devastating hurricane kills 392.

1934 Pan Am Airlines begins passenger flights between Miami and Latin America, forging the city's "Gateway of the Americas" tag.

1941 Empty tourist hotels in Miami Beach become barracks for troops during World War II.

1965 The first "freedom flight" from Havana lands. Such flights bring 230,000 Cubans to Miami.

1979 South Beach's Art Deco District is added to the National Register of Historic Places.

1980 The "Mariel Boatlift" brings a further 125,000 Cubans to Miami. Riots erupt following the acquittal of white police officers accused of assaulting a black insurance salesman.

1984 First broadcast of *Miami Vice*. The popular TV cop show underlines Miami's warm climate and uses its best architecture as a backdrop.

1992 Hurricane Andrew kills 53 people and destroys 158,000 homes. The damage is assessed at $30 billion.

1997 Fashion designer Gianni Versace is fatally shot outside his Ocean Drive home.

1999 Custody battle over Elian Gonzalez.

2000 Elian Gonzalez returns with his father to Cuba.

PEOPLE & EVENTS FROM HISTORY

Carl Fisher

Car headlight mogul Carl Fisher, famous for building the Indianapolis Speedway, moved to Miami in 1912 and began viewing the barrier island dividing Biscayne Bay from the ocean with an entrepreneur's eye. Fisher financed the world's longest wooden bridge to link the island to Miami, then built the luxury resorts that made 1920s Miami Beach—as the island was now titled—a socialites' playground. His $50 million fortune wiped out by the Depression, Fisher died in 1936, $4 million in debt.

THE LAND BOOM

Many middle-class citizens headed to Miami in the economically buoyant years that followed World War I, envisioning vast profits and luxurious lifestyles from buying land. In the first half of the 1920s Miami's population quadrupled, and land values sometimes tripled within a day. Some developments, such as Coral Gables, were properly planned. By 1925, however, rogue agents were selling useless plots of land on a "site unseen" basis to desperate buyers. By late 1926 the boom was over, 40 city banks had closed, and a hurricane compounded the city's woes.

ART-DECO PRESERVATION

Throughout the 1930s hotels and other buildings were built in the South Beach section of Miami Beach, to stimulate a tourist boom and help the local economy recover from the Depression. The 800 or so buildings were raised in the fashionable style of the day: art deco. With porthole windows, streamlined features, bas-reliefs, and tropical motifs, the buildings took on a unique look, subsequently termed Miami Beach Art Deco. Launched in 1976, the Miami Design Preservation League overcame considerable opposition to have the area placed on the National Register of Historic Places in 1979, and encouraged the restoration and remodeling of the buildings.

HURRICANE ANDREW

Gusting at 168 miles per hour, Hurricane Andrew slammed into Miami on August 24, 1992, the biggest to strike the city since 1937. Jumbo jets at Miami Airport were overturned, moored yachts were carried inland, roofs were torn from buildings. Fifty-three people died, while 158,000 homes, 59 hospitals, and nine schools were destroyed. Some 250,000 people were rendered homeless, and damage was assessed at $30 billion.

Hit by Andrew

MIAMI
how to organize your time

ITINERARIES

Although the city as a whole covers a large area, much of Miami Beach and several parts of Miami itself can be explored easily and safely on foot. The city's buses, and to a lesser extent the single-route Metrorail system, can link individual sights and neighborhoods worth seeing: getting between Downtown and Miami Beach is very convenient.

ITINERARY ONE	**MIAMI BEACH & SOUTH BEACH**
Morning	Explore the expansive public areas and lavish gardens of the Fontainebleau Hotel (➤ 48). Take the Boardwalk to 21st Street. Visit the Bass Museum of Art (➤ 47) and continue the few blocks to Lincoln Road for lunch.
Lunch	El Viajante Segundo (➤ 66) for a taste of Cuba, or Van Dyke Café (➤ 69).
Afternoon	Continue to South Beach. Explore the art-deco buildings of Washington and Collins avenues and Ocean Drive. Visit the Wolfsonian (➤ 45) and the Jewish Museum of Florida (➤ 46).
ITINERARY TWO	**DOWNTOWN & VIZCAYA**
Morning	Visit the Historical Museum of Southern Florida (➤ 37) and continue to the Federal Courthouse (➤ 38).
Lunch	Granny Feelgood's (➤ 17) for a budget meal or Fishbone Grill (➤ 65).
Afternoon	Travel by bus or Metrorail to Vizcaya (➤ 36). With children, the neighboring Museum of Science (➤ 35) might be a better option. If time remains, walk to the Cuban church, Ermita de la Caridad (➤ 60).
ITINERARY THREE	**CORAL GABLES**
Morning	Tour the public areas of Coral Gables City Hall (➤ 31) and explore the stores and architecture around the Miracle Mile. Walk west along Coral Way to Coral Gables Merrick House (➤ 28).
Lunch	JohnMartin's (➤ 83) for classy Irish food, or House of India (➤ 68) for a buffet. For a snack,

	stop at the café in the Barnes & Noble book-store (▶ 75).
Afternoon	Walk south to the Venetian Pool (▶ 29), continuing to Coral Gables Congregational Church (▶ 56) and the Biltmore Hotel (▶ 26). Explore the hotel's public areas and admire the immense pool.
ITINERARY FOUR	**COCONUT GROVE & KEY BISCAYNE**
Morning	Tour the CocoWalk (▶ 70) and Streets of Mayfair (▶ 71) shopping malls, and the many one-of-a-kind shops in the neighborhood. Walk along Main Highway to the Barnacle (▶ 33). Make the longer walk or short taxi ride to Plymouth Congregational Church (▶ 32).
Lunch	Spanish food and more at Café Tù-Tu Tango (✉ CocoWalk, 3015 Grand Avenue ☎ 305/529-2222), or Mexican fare at Señor Frog's Mexican Grill (▶ 67).
Afternoon	Take the downtown bus and transfer to the Key Biscayne bus. Picnic with a view at Crandon Park (▶ 52), or watch the aquatic shows at Miami Seaquarium (▶ 55). Continue through the residential area to reach the expansive Bill Baggs Cape Florida State Recreation Area (▶ 43). Walk Cape Florida's boardwalk and have a look at the 19th-century Cape Florida lighthouse.

Key Biscayne

WALKS

Strolling South Beach

THE SIGHTS

- The Cardozo,
  1300 Ocean Drive
- The Carlyle,
  1250 Ocean Drive
- The Leslie,
  1244 Ocean Drive
- The Colony,
  736 Ocean Drive

INFORMATION

Distance 2–3 miles
Time 2–4 hours
Start point Boardwalk
➕ N2–5
🚌 C, H
End point 6th Street
➕ M7
🚌 C, F/M, H, K, S

16

THE BOARDWALK

Miami Beach's Boardwalk runs between the beach and the ocean-view hotels and condominiums lining Collins Avenue. Accessed from any adjoining street, the Boardwalk is used by locals for exercise and dog walking. The Boardwalk runs between 46th and 21st streets, with shaded "resting points" and bench seats at regular intervals. The views across the ocean and the beach are splendid. The grounds of several hotels provide access to the Boardwalk, and their cafés and bars make convenient lunch stops. The most illustrious is the Trop-Art Café of the Fontainebleau (➤ 48). Away from the Boardwalk, try Van Dyke Café (➤ 69), or the Cuban food of El Viajante Segundo (➤ 66).

Art Deco District An eight-block walk or bus ride from 21st Street carries you into the heart of South Beach's Art Deco District. For the most dramatic architectural view, Ocean Drive has many of the most evocatively remodeled buildings, gleaming with pastel colors and full of eye-catching decoration. Many of these are hotels with lobbies open to the public. Heading south, finish at Park Central and its mezzanine level historical display. Other architectural landmarks within an easy stroll include the Beach Patrol Station on the beach itself and, on Washington Avenue, the Miami Beach Post Office, built in 1937 and crowned by a marble and stained-glass lantern.

DOWNTOWN & BAYSIDE MARKETPLACE

Along with the office high-rises of nearby Brickell Avenue, downtown Miami is the business hub of the city and is largely deserted at night. Lined by a mixture of stately 1920s buildings and undistinguished modern structures, Downtown's streets also give access to numerous mini-shopping malls that serve an almost exclusively Spanish-speaking clientele. Start at the Philip Johnson-designed Metro-Dade Cultural Center, which has the Historical Museum of Southern Florida, the Miami Art

Museum of Dade County, and the city's main public library, grouped around a delightful sun-drenched plaza. Nearby is the distinctive Miami-Dade County Courthouse, built between 1925 and 1928 in neo-classical style. Continue south along N.E. 1st Street and turn left along N.E. 1st Avenue. This route passes the beautiful 1920s Gesu Catholic Church and reaches the combined old and new Federal Courthouse.

Lunch Inside Government Center, reached by a walkway from the Metro-Dade Cultural Center, are several food counters offering affordable snacks and meals. Nearby is Granny Feelgood's (✉ 25 W. Flagler Street ☎ 305/377-9600) and the inexpensive Royal Palm Café (✉ 22 E. Flagler Street ☎ 305/577-2420). Bayside Marketplace also has a food court as well as several restaurants, including the pricey but highly regarded Nicaraguan favorite, Los Ranchos (➤ 67).

Two blocks south of the courthouse lies busy Biscayne Boulevard. Here, the Spanish-influenced Freedom Tower is clearly visible. Take a closer look at the tower, then cross Biscayne Boulevard to Bayside Marketplace, an indoor shopping mall of more than 140 stores, restaurants, and attractions, and a departure point for city boat tours.

THE SIGHTS

- Historical Museum of Southern Florida (➤ 37)
- Miami Art Museum of Dade County (➤ 54)
- Dade County Courthouse (➤ 56)
- Federal Courthouse (➤ 38)
- Bayside Marketplace (➤ 70)

INFORMATION

Distance About 2 miles
Time 2–3 hours
Start point Metro-Dade Cultural Center
🚇 E/F 7/8
🚊 Government Center
🚌 All serving Downtown Miami
End point Bayside Marketplace
🚇 G7
🚌 3, 16, 48, 95 C, S

Biscayne Boulevard

17

EVENINGS OUT

Bayside Marketplace

Most areas of Miami have their share of restaurants, bars, and nightspots, but by far the most numerous—and the most chic—are in South Beach, also a place unmatched for casual evening walks. Otherwise, only Coconut Grove is worth visiting simply for idle after-dark strolls.

SOUTH BEACH

The heart of the Art Deco District and a hangout for fashion models and their admirers, South Beach has a monopoly on Miami's zestiest nightlife. Stroll Ocean Drive, where cooling breezes wash in from the sea and neon-lit, art-deco hotels often have a trendy restaurant—and equally trendy clientele—spilling onto the sidewalk. Open-air poolside bars are common and, just inland, Collins and Washington avenues are home to numerous budgetwise restaurants and hole-in-the-wall bars and clubs patronized by celebrities and locals alike. Socially, South Beach does not warm up until midnight and continues to party well into the early hours. Many clubs and bars stay open until 5AM.

COCONUT GROVE

Around the junction of Grand Avenue and Main Highway, Coconut Grove contains a plethora of browse-worthy stores that stay open late and numerous restaurants and cafés that, in the evening, serve a predominantly local crowd. Though less fashionable than South Beach, Coconut Grove regularly attracts a fair complement of stylish Miamians and celebrities, some of them with apartments in the neighborhood's growing number of high-rise, huge-rent towers. Be cautious if using the Coconut Grove Metrorail station, which is several blocks from the nightlife area—keep to well-lit, busy streets and do not take short cuts through dark alleys.

INFORMATION

South Beach
✚ M6/7
▤ C, H, K, W, S

Coconut Grove
✚ Off map
▣ Coconut Grove
▤ 42, 48

ORGANIZED SIGHTSEEING

WALKING TOURS

Art Deco District ☎ 305/672-2014
90-minute Saturday morning and Thursday evening strolls around the best of South Beach's art-deco architecture.

Dr. George's Tours ☎ 305/375-1492
A respected Historical Museum of Southern Florida employee leads these tours, which focus on under-explored quarters, such as Little Havana and the Miami Cemetery.

BOAT TOURS

Casino Precesa ☎ 305/379-LUCK
Daily evening, and late-night gambling cruises. Options aboard range from slot machines to black jack. You must be at least 21 and the fare includes a light buffet.

Dr. George's Tours ☎ 305/375-1492
Besides walking tours, Dr. George leads boat trips with commentary along the Miami River and across Biscayne Bay.

Miami River Historical Jungle Tours ☎ 305/755-9055
Daily voyages across Biscayne Bay and along parts of the Miami River revealing much about the natural and social history of the city.

Ocean Drive art deco

Water Taxi ☎ 954/467-6677
An enjoyable scheduled service across Biscayne Bay between downtown and Miami Beach. Single-trip and all-day passes available.

AIR TOURS

Action Helicopter ☎ 305/358-1788
Swooping over Miami in a helicopter is an exhilarating way to live out *Miami Vice* fantasies. All-day charter available.

Pan Am Air Bridge ☎ 800/371-2330
Low-level hops across Miami on a seaplane, or longer flights to the Florida Keys or the Bahamas.

BICYCLE TOURS

Art Deco District ☎ 305/672-2014
The cream of South Beach's architecture viewed from a bicycle. Tours leave from Cycles on the Beach ✉ 713 5th Street every Sunday; fees include bike rental.

19

Excursions

INFORMATION

Biscayne National Park
Entrance Eastern end of S.W. 328th Street
☎ 305/230-7275
Distance 26 miles from Downtown Miami
Public transportation None

Everglades National Park
Entrance State Road 9336
☎ 305/242-7700
Distance 35 miles from Downtown Miami; from main entrance to Flamingo, 38 miles
Public transportation None

The Everglades

BISCAYNE NATIONAL PARK

Biscayne National Park fills 181,000 undersea acres between the southern reaches of Miami and Key Largo, the first island of the Florida Keys. The park protects part of the series of coral reefs that continue for 100 miles south, providing a habitat for a colorful collection of marine life and scattered with the wrecked vessels of early European explorers and traders. Numerous guided snorkeling, scuba diving, and boat trips are available, and you can also view the reef from a glass-bottomed boat.

EVERGLADES NATIONAL PARK

The Everglades, a vast "river of grass," lies southwest of Miami. Although only the 8 million acres south of Lake Okeechobee are protected as a national park, the remarkable ecosystem extends much farther and is continually threatened by southern Florida's rapid urban development. The Everglades change considerably between the wet summer season, when the area provides drainage between Lake Okeechobee and the ocean, and the dry winter season, when the wildlife is at its most abundant. The park's main entrance is on the SR 9336, the main road through the park. Close by is the Royal Palm Visitor Center, which provides basic information on the unique combination of terrain, climate, vegetation, and wildlife that underpins Everglades life. At regular points off the road, clearly marked foot trails probe slightly deeper and are likely to bring views of roseate spoonbills and alligators, unerring in their ability to detect water during the dry winter. Flamingo, the former pioneer settlement where the road ends, is the site of Flamingo Lodge, the park's only hotel.

NORTH TO PALM BEACH

Head north by car from Miami Beach on Highway A1A and the reward is not only almost constant ocean views but, within a few hours, passing through three of southern Florida's most distinctive communities.

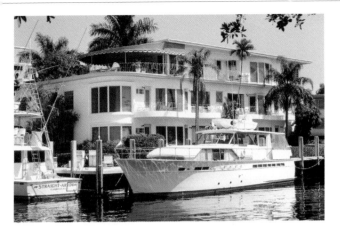

Fort Lauderdale

At Fort Lauderdale, the highway charts a course between a lengthy beach lined by hotels and lively restaurants and bars, and a series of canals that weave around artificial islands with million-dollar homes. Visit the International Swimming Hall of Fame, where memorabilia of U.S. champion swimmers and divers occupies a stunning complex, and the 1919 Bonnet House, a 30-room plantation-style home on 35 acres. Inland are the Museum of Art, housing modern pieces, and the child-friendly Museum of Discovery & Science.

Farther north is Mediterranean-style Boca Raton. Its architecture—red tiled roofs, mock bell towers, and loggias—is no accident. The community was created during the 1920s' land boom by self-made architect Addison Mizner, who also designed much of Palm Beach, including the rambling Boca Raton building; restrictions on new construction perpetuate the look.

Palm Beach is a playground of the rich and famous. Explore the pricey stores along Worth Avenue and the many Mizner-designed court-yards that lead off it. To discover the secluded northern part of Palm Beach, site of its most expensive homes, walk or cycle the 3-mile lake-front trail exempt from automobiles. Bicycle rentals are available at Palm Beach Bicycle Trail Shop ✉ 223 Sunrise Avenue.

INFORMATION

Palm Beach
Distance 64 miles
Start point Miami Beach
Public transportation None

Greater Fort Lauderdale
Convention & Visitors Bureau
✉ 1850 Eller Drive, Suite 303, Fort Lauderdale
☎ 800/356-1662 or 800/22-SUNNY

Boca Raton Chamber of Commerce
✉ 1800 N. Dixie Highway, Boca Raton
☎ 561/395-4433

Palm Beach Chamber of Commerce
✉ 45 Cocoanut Row, Palm Beach
☎ 561/655-3282

WHAT'S ON

Something is always happening in Miami, although the peak time for events is October to March. *Greater Miami & the Beaches Visitors Guide* is published twice-yearly by the city's Convention & Visitors Bureau ⊠ 701 Brickell Avenue. Also consult the Friday edition of the *Miami Herald*, and the free weekly newspaper, *New Times*.

January	*Orange Bowl*: Culmination of the college football season. *Art-Deco Weekend*: Walks, talks, and other events celebrate South Beach's architecture.
February	*Miami Film Festival*: Ten days of independent movies, most from North, South, and Central America.
March	*Carnaval Miami*: Little Havana's colorful celebration of Cuban culture with floats, food stands, and dancing.
April	*Merrick Festival*: Coral Gables salutes its founder with numerous historically themed events.
May	*Arabian Nights Festival*: Opa-locka marks its pseudo-Middle Eastern architecture with events around Opa-locka City Hall.
June	*Goombay Festival*: Caribbean music, food, and much more in Coconut Grove's Peacock Park.
July	*America's Birthday Bash*: Bayfront Park is the focus of the city's Independence Day revelries.
August	*Miami Reggae Festival*: Top reggae names appear over two days in Downtown's Bicentennial Park.
September	*Festival Miami*: Four weeks of performing-arts events at the University of Miami; continues into October.
October	*Columbus Day Regatta*: A small armada of yachts races out of Key Biscayne.
November	*Miami Book Fair*: Major event for international publishers and authors; open to the public.

MIAMI's
top 25 sights

The sights are shown on the maps on the inside front cover and inside back cover, numbered **1–25** *from west to east across the city*

MIAMI METROZOO

HIGHLIGHTS

- Komodo dragons
- Bengal tigers
- Koalas
- Bentang
- Indian muntjac
- Asian and African elephants
- Siamese crocodiles
- Himalayan black bear
- Sable antelope
- Wattled crane

INFORMATION

- ✚ Off map
- ✉ 12400 S.W. 152nd Street
- ☎ 305/251-0400
- ◷ Daily 9:30–5:30
- 🍴 Fast-food areas
- 🚌 Zoo Express, from Dadeland North
- ♿ Good
- 💰 Moderate
- 🔗 Gold Coast Railroad Museum (➤ 54)

Below: A Bengal tiger

Spread across 290 cageless acres at Miami's southernmost reaches, the Metrozoo offers a rare chance to see white tigers, Komodo dragons, koalas, crocodiles, elephants, and many more creatures from every corner of the globe.

Special creatures With fewer than 100 believed to be in existence and none remaining in the wild, the zoo's prowling white Bengal tigers, with their white fur and blue eyes, make a spectacular beginning to your zoo visit. No less memorable are the cuddly koalas, not to mention the adult pair of Komodo dragons, native to Indonesia and brought to the zoo in 1996. The largest and most powerful species of lizard, the Komodo dragon is a ferocious predator with a virulent bacterium in its mouth to fatally infect its prey.

Special corners Along the 3-mile pathway that links the various enclosures are several walk-in viewing "caves," imitation rock tunnels that lead to concealed windows that let you spy on creatures such as orangutans and gorillas. Another special section, Asian River Life, brings together assorted lizards, small-clawed Asian river otters, a clouded leopard, and several Indian muntjac—an antlered Asian deer growing to only about 40 inches in height and known for barking at its enemies. Regular, informative presentations on the animals and their lives take place at the amphitheater, and at feeding times the zoo keepers are happy to talk about their charges. There's also a special area for kids named PAWS and an elevated railway runs through the park.

CORAL CASTLE

Nobody knows quite how he did it, but when Latvian émigré Edward Leedskalnin created the Coral Castle as a tribute to his lost love, he gave Miami one of its strangest and longest-lasting places of interest.

Loser in love Jilted by his 16-year-old would-be bride, the broken-hearted Leedskalnin left Latvia for North America, roaming the continent, then settling around 1920 in southern Florida where he bought an acre of land for $12. He began raising chunks of coral rock from the ground and making the bulky sculptures, most resembling over-sized pieces of furniture, that steadily evolved into an outdoor garden known as the Coral Castle, presumed to be a memorial to his unrequited love. Today you can see Leedskalnin's threadbare but comfortable living quarters and workshop and far more dramatic, the dozens of sculptures themselves. They include the 9-ton Gate, which is so well balanced that it can be opened by finger pressure; the 1,000-pound rock chairs that gently pivot back and forth; a 2-ton Valentine heart; and the Florida Table, its shape and dimensions exactly proportionate to those of the state.

Mysteries Nobody ever saw Leedskalnin working, and how he carved the heavy and extremely hard coral using only hand tools is a mystery. Nor could anyone deduce how he could move pieces of rock weighing several tons without assistance. Also amazing was his knowledge of astronomy and astrology, reflected by the 25-foot-tall Polaris Telescope, aimed at the North Star and used to make calculations for Leedskalnin's Sundial, and to research the sculptural representations of Mars and Saturn, and the much-photographed Crescent Moon.

DID YOU KNOW?

Edward Leedskalnin
- Born: Latvia 1887
- Age when jilted: 26
- Height: 5 feet
- Weight: 100 pounds
- Coral Castle construction: 1920–1940
- Previous jobs in U.S.: lumberman, cowboy
- Died: Miami 1951

INFORMATION

- Off map
- 28655 S. Dixie Highway
- 305/248-6345
- Daily 9–7
- 35, 70
- Few
- Moderate

Leedskalnin's kitchen

3

THE BILTMORE HOTEL

Few buildings encapsulate the glamour of 1920s Miami better than the Biltmore Hotel, created at the height of the property boom and the Florida stomping ground of the rich and famous during that carefree golden era.

Opulent openings Touted as "the last word in the evolution of civilization, the acme of hostelries and clubs," the Biltmore opened in 1926 to pamper a train-load of celebrities from New York. Boasting Italian marble, 8-foot-high crystal chandeliers, and an 18-hole golf course, the hotel was created by the architectural firm of Schultze & Weaver, later renowned for New York's scene-setting Waldorf-Astoria Hotel. Biltmore guests were kept amused by tennis, fox-hunting, horseback-riding, and fashion shows, and fed on pheasant and trout. They could dip in the mammoth-sized pool under the eye of swimming instructor Johnny Weissmuller, future Olympic champion and Hollywood's most popular Tarzan.

Biltmore today The 1926 hurricane and the Depression ended the Biltmore's days of luxury, but throughout the 1980s the hotel was expensively restored. The elegance begins as you enter the lobby, topped by a vaulted ceiling and marked at one end by an enormous fireplace and leering gargoyles. Through the lobby you pass by the dining rooms into an exquisitely tiled terrace loggia, where you can gaze out across the golf course and the pool. The hotel's tower, modeled on Spain's Giralda and rising 26 stories, holds the most expensive guest rooms and the so-called Al Capone suite, said to be haunted by the ghost of the legendary gangster's bodyguard, slain here while on duty.

LOWE ART MUSEUM

The Lowe Art Museum has long held a remarkable collection of European art. It has more recently acquired a reputation for its Native American collections and imaginative temporary exhibitions of classic and contemporary work.

Eclectic collections Opened in 1950, the museum was the first art institution in the Miami area. A significant early benefactor was Samuel H. Kress, whose family bequeathed the substantial stock of predominantly Renaissance and baroque art that still provides the core of the permanent European holdings. Among many notable works on view are the 14th-century *Madonna and Child Enthroned With Donors and Saints Dominic and Elizabeth of Hungary*, by the Sienese Lippo Vanni, one of the few altarpieces painted in Naples during the period of French royal rule; the entertaining 1650s *The Trapped Thief*, attributed to Van Galen; and works by later luminaries such as Thomas Gainsborough and Paul Gauguin.

American art A broad sweep of U.S. art reaches from the 19th-century large-scale depictions of the American West by Albert Bierstadt and the mystically charged Florida landscapes of George Inness, to modern works by Frank Stella, Roy Liechtenstein, and Duane Hanson, represented by his uncannily lifelike *College Football Player*. Expansion plans call for more space for an absorbing Native American collection, which includes a Haida halibut hook, made from wood and bone, a 19th-century Tlinglet frontlet headdress, a Zuni pueblo jar from around 1875 decorated with a deer design, and a set of imposing 1920s color lithographs of Florida's Seminole chiefs.

HIGHLIGHTS

- Lakota woman's dress
- *Madonna and Child Enthroned With Donors and Saints Dominic and Elizabeth of Hungary*, Lippo Vanni
- Anasazi effigy vessel
- *College Football Player*, Duane Hanson

INFORMATION

- Off map
- 1301 Stanford Drive, University of Miami
- 305/284-3535
- Tue, Wed, Fri, Sat 10–5; Thu noon–7; Sun noon–5
- University
- 48, 52, 72
- Good
- Inexpensive
- Biltmore Hotel (➤ 26), Coral Gables City Hall (➤ 31), Coral Gables Merrick House (➤ 28), Venetian Pool (➤ 29)

Top: The Adultress Before Christ, *Rocco Marconi*
Below: Tall vase exhibit

5

CORAL GABLES MERRICK HOUSE

George Merrick planned the "city beautiful" of Coral Gables, one of the few aesthetic successes of the 1920s Miami land boom; his boyhood home is an essential stop for anyone captivated by the neighborhood's architecture and intrigued by Merrick himself.

Early days Coral Gables Merrick House dates from 1899 and began as a simple woodframe home for the Merrick family, including the young George, and an administrative base for running their citrus and vegetable farm. The farm became the site of the city of Coral Gables, and the house expanded into the spacious residence of coral-rock walls and red-tiled gabled roof that remains today. The rebuilding resulted from the prosperity of the farm and the desire of George's mother to live in a Southern-style plantation home.

Looking inside An introductory video provides the background to the house and to George Merrick's later achievements, describing many of the distinguishing architectural features of the new city, some of which are represented in the house. Innumerable furnishings and ornaments, such as a grand piano and grandfather clock, are thought to be from the Merrick family's time, and the aging typewriter was used in farm correspondence. Many family photographs and enthusiastic though amateurish paintings by Mrs Merrick decorate the house. Economic hardship following the 1926 property crash caused the building to be converted into apartments known as Merrick Manor. Complete decline was only halted by its sale to a historically minded local in 1966 and the restoration that began in 1977.

VENETIAN POOL

With its pseudo-Venetian lampposts, dainty cobblestoned bridges, cypress-roofed loggias, porticoes, palm trees, and three-story observation towers, few swimming pools anywhere in the world can match the architectural exuberance of the Venetian Pool.

Looking good   The quarrying of rock to build Coral Gables during the 1920s left a very large hole in the ground which, in keeping with the ingenuity that underpinned the creation of the city, was transformed into the majestic Venetian Pool. Intended to spare local residents the sight of an ugly limestone quarry, the pool was completed in 1924 and designed, like much of Coral Gables, by George Merrick's uncle, artist Denman Fink, and architect Phineas Paist. In its early years, the pool not only provided locals with a place to cool off but, with the drained pool functioning as an amphitheater, staged beauty contests and concerts.

Making a splash   Further entertainment was provided by the "water shows" of five-times Olympic swimming gold medalist (and future Tarzan) Johnny Weissmuller and swimmer-actress Esther Williams, and the lectures given by the larger-than-life orator and former politician William Jennings Bryan, praising Coral Gables to the skies in return for an annual cash salary of $50,000. The pool remains an extremely attractive and pleasant place to swim. Weekdays, outside school vacations, are particularly free of crowds. Until 1986, the pool was filled naturally from an artesian well, its 800,000 gallons drained nightly and replaced each morning. Nowadays, the water is recycled using natural ground filtration.

DID YOU KNOW?

Phineas Paist
- 1875: Born in Franklin, Pennsylvania
- 1916: Arrives Miami, consultant on Vizcaya
- 1920: Appointed supervising architect of Coral Gables Corporation
- 1926: Construction begins on Paist's first building for University of Miami; interrupted by hurricane, building is completed 20 years later

Denman Fink
- 1881: Born in Springdale, Pennsylvania
- 1920: Appointed art director, Coral Gables Corporation
- 1925: Joins faculty of University of Miami
- 1952: Retires, then head of Miami University Art Department

INFORMATION

- ✚ Off map
- ✉ 2701 De Soto Boulevard
- ☎ 305/460-5356
- 🕐 Tue–Fri 11–5:30; Sat–Sun 10–4:30. Closed Mon
- 🚌 24, 72
- ♿ Few
- 💲 Moderate
- ↔ Biltmore Hotel (➤ 26), Coral Gables Merrick House (➤ 28), Lowe Art Museum (➤ 27)

7

FAIRCHILD TROPICAL GARDEN

DID YOU KNOW?

- Endangered plant species grown: 412
- Palm species: 889
- Palms in the ground: 3,465
- Lakes: 11

David Fairchild

- 1869: Born
- 1896: First visit to tropics
- 1916: Moves into Kampong, a landmark Coconut Grove home. Planted with tropical and other exotic plants, Kampong's 7.5-acre gardens draw botany students from across the United States
- 1954: Dies

INFORMATION

- ✚ Off map
- ✉ 10901 Old Cutler Road
- ☎ 305/667-1651
- ◷ Daily 9:30–4:30
- 🍴 Café
- ▣ 65
- ♿ Good
- 🎫 Moderate
- ↔ Matheson Hammock Park (➤ 52)
- ❓ Many weekend special events

Southern Florida is the only place in the continental United States where subtropical and tropical plants can grow outdoors year-round; Fairchild Tropical Garden provides a reminder of the natural life of Florida and beyond.

Germination Built during the Depression by the Civilian Conservation Corps (CCC), Fairchild Tropical Garden has been open to the public since 1938. The gardens bear the name of distinguished botanist David Fairchild, a prominent tropical botanist and resident of Miami whose life's work was to bring examples of tropical plants to the United States. The 83-acre garden—designed by American landscape artist William Lyman Phillips—not only showcases tropical plantlife but runs numerous educational programs. Many miles of pathway weave through the gardens beside beautiful lakes—a positive side-effect of the CCC's "make-work" strategy—but the most useful overview is provided by the 40-minute narrated tram tour of the garden, which is included in the admission price.

Tropical things Among the wealth of palms, bromeliads, cycads, vines, and much more, are oddities such as the baobab, an African tree which achieves astonishing lateral growth with branches as thick as most trees' trunks, and the aromatic ylang-ylang tree, oil from whose blossoms are used in Chanel No.5 perfume. In the Window to the Tropics conservatory, 16,000sq feet of exhibits and displays explore the complex and threatened ecology of the world's rain forests, providing stark evidence of the ongoing destruction. The garden's 1939 gatehouse, constructed from local coral rock, is a museum of plant exploration.

CORAL GABLES CITY HALL

Nowhere is the Mediterranean style of Coral Gables shown to better effect than at City Hall, a building raised in Spanish Renaissance style that still forms an eye-catching centerpiece to the area it serves.

From despair While much of Coral Gables was planned and built in the buoyant years of the Miami land boom, City Hall arose in the sober and depressed times that followed the collapse of the property market. Financed by a bond issue, the building was completed in 1928 within a mere four months for a modest $200,000, yet it encapsulates much that is good about Coral Gables' love affair with Mediterranean architecture. Overlooking the showpiece business and shopping strip of the Miracle Mile is City Hall's semicircular eastern wing, with its facade of 12 columns supporting a cornice bearing the Coral Gables coat of arms. Emerging from the top of the pile is a three-tiered Spanish Renaissance-style clock tower from which passing hours are marked by the chimes of a 500-pound bell.

To celebration Inside, City Hall continues to fulfill its administrative function, and many of its narrow, atmospheric corridors are decorated with memorabilia from the community's past, including photographs of the Biltmore Hotel taken during its heyday in the late 1920s. Be sure to look up from the second-floor landing at the impressive Denman Fink mural depicting the four seasons that decorates the tower's domed ceiling. The office of the Department of Historic Preservation holds many of Coral Gables' early plans and dispenses a wealth of historical information and interesting literature about the city.

DID YOU KNOW?

Coral Gables
- Population: 41,406
- Area: 11.96sq miles
- Schools: 7 public, 4 private
- Businesses: 7,509
- Parkland: 40 acres
- Golf courses: 2
- Tennis courts: 25
- Households: 15,741

INFORMATION

- ✛ Off map
- ✉ 405 Biltmore Way
- ☎ 305/446-6800
- 🕐 Best to visit Mon–Fri 9–5; closed holidays. Hours vary, call to check
- 🚍 24, 40, 56, 73, J
- ♿ Good
- 🆓 Free
- ↔ Biltmore Hotel (➤ 26), Coral Gables Merrick House (➤ 28), Lowe Art Museum (➤ 27), Venetian Pool (➤ 29)

Top: The Colonnade

9

PLYMOUTH CONGREGATIONAL CHURCH

INFORMATION

➕ Off map

✉ 3400 Devon Road

☎ 305/444-6521

🕐 Hours vary but the church can be unlocked for visits; telephone before arrival

🚌 48

♿ Few

💲 Free

↔ Barnacle State Historic Site (➤ 33), Museum of Science (➤ 35), Vizcaya Museum and Gardens (➤ 36)

The ivy-cloaked stone Plymouth Congregational Church is just a few minutes' drive from Coconut Grove's fashionable stores and restaurants, but it seems as if it belongs in medieval Europe.

Beginnings The origins of Plymouth Congregational Church reach back to 1897, when the religious needs of the isolated settlement of Coconut Grove were served by a small wooden chapel. By 1916 the current church was under construction, loosely modeled on a city mission church in Mexico. Incredibly, the church's distinguished stonework was built by a Spanish mason working alone, and using no tools other than a T-square, hatchet, trowel, and plumb-line. The church was completed in 1917; its main entrance is marked by an oak-backed walnut door with wrought-iron fittings that originally belonged to a monastery in the Pyrenees and is claimed to be nearly 400 years old.

Expansion One feature of the door that is not original is the hole cut into the lower right-hand corner. This allows easy entry for cats, who keep down the church's population of mice. As Coconut Grove grew, so too did the church's congregation and many of the interior features were donated by the area's increasingly affluent residents. Two transepts and a new chancel, forming the church into the shape of the Cross, were added in 1954. Outside, the attractive grounds include a Memorial Garden.

Detail above entrance

BARNACLE STATE HISTORIC SITE

Few pioneer dwellings are as ingenious or as well preserved as the Barnacle, erected by a sea-loving Massachusetts boat designer who was once Coconut Grove's earliest and most influential resident.

Arrival Described as "the catalyst that brought Coconut Grove into being," Ralph Middleton Munroe, a naval architect and photographer known as "The Commodore," first visited the nascent Coconut Grove in 1881, hoping the climate would improve the health of his wife, Eva, ill with tuberculosis. He befriended Charles and Isabella Peacock, future owners of Miami's, and southern Florida's, first hotel. The Peacocks encouraged Munroe to make the area his home by giving him 4 acres of land. Buying a further 40 acres of bayside property, Munroe returned permanently in 1891 and built what became known as the Barnacle as his home.

Settlement Munroe earned a national reputation designing shallow-draft vessels for the treacherous waters around Florida's coast. With the Barnacle, he also showed considerable skills in domestic building. Raised above ground to improve air flow and prevent flooding, the Barnacle has a veranda to provide shade and shelter, and a skylight opened by pulleys to improve air circulation. Coated with oil to deter termites, the pine posts that anchor the Barnacle to the ground also helped it survive the devastating hurricanes of 1926 and 1992. Most ingeniously of all, Munroe created extra living space in 1908 by raising the Barnacle above ground and building an additional story under the original one. In 1973, Munroe's surviving children resisted offers from developers for the Barnacle and its land, and sold it to the state of Florida for protection as a State Historic Site.

DID YOU KNOW?

Ralph Middleton Munroe

- 1877: Makes first visit to southern Florida
- 1881: Visits Coconut Grove
- 1887: Co-founds the Biscayne Bay Yacht Club
- 1890: Opens area's first sawmill; wood salvaged from shipwrecks is used in building the Barnacle
- 1891: Donates land for building of Union Chapel
- 1930: Publication of Munroe's autobiographical *The Commodore's Story*
- 1933: Dies aged 82, buried in hometown of Concord, Massachusetts

INFORMATION

- ✚ Off map
- ✉ 3485 Main Highway
- ☎ 305/448-9445
- ⏰ Guided tours Fri–Sun 10, 11:30, 1, and 2:30; grounds open during daylight hours
- 🚌 42, 48
- ♿ Few
- 💰 Inexpensive
- ↔ Plymouth Congregational Church (➤ 32), Museum of Science (➤ 35), Vizcaya Museum and Gardens (➤ 36)

BRIGADE 2506 MEMORIAL

DID YOU KNOW?

- 1959: Miami's prerevolution Cuban population is 10,000
- 1960: 45,000 Cuban refugees arrive in Miami
- 1965–1973: "Freedom flights" bring in 230,000 Cubans
- 1974: 400,000 Cubans in Miami
- 1980: 125,000 arrive from Cuba on "Freedom Flotilla"
- 1984: Cubans form 42 percent of Miami's population
- 1996: 600,000 Cubans in Miami

INFORMATION

- C9
- Junction of S.W. 8th Street and S.W. 13th Avenue
- Always open
- 8, 12
- Good
- Free
- Cuban Museum of The Americas (➤ 54), José Martí Park (➤ 52), Máximo Gómez Park (➤ 52)

Cubans, and people of Cuban descent, form a substantial part of Miami's population and leave few people in doubt of their antipathy towards Cuba's political regime, a feeling evoked most strongly at Little Havana's Brigade 2506 Memorial.

Cuban exile When revolution ousted the Batista dictatorship and Fidel Castro took power in Cuba in 1959, he had widespread support throughout the country. Nonetheless, many wealthy Cubans left immediately for the United States and many more fled the new regimes abuses in subsequent years. A 50-minute flight away, Miami—which had long sheltered Cubans in exile—was the obvious destination. Reflecting U.S. opposition to the Castro administration, the CIA trained and equipped a would-be Cuban invasion force of former soldiers, mercenaries, politicians, and idealistic young exiles, which became known as Brigade 2506. In April 1961, the 1,300-strong brigade landed at Cuba's Bahía de Cochinos (Bay of Pigs). With U.S. support withdrawn and many in Cuba denouncing its members as traitors, the brigade was swiftly repelled by Castro's troops: 80 were killed, 37 drowned and the remainder taken prisoner, later returned to the U.S. in exchange for food and medicines.

The Memorial Draped by the Cuban flag, the memorial has an eternal flame and plaques with the names of those who died, and marks the start of a tree-lined promenade dotted with markers to Cuban heroes such as writer and independence campaigner José Martí.

Memorial statue

MUSEUM OF SCIENCE

Since its founding in 1949, the Museum of Science has informed and entertained by unraveling some of the mysteries and wonders of the natural world, with many hands-on exhibits, a wildlife center, and a top-class planetarium.

Permanent exhibits Investigations into sound, light, and gravity, dioramas of natural Florida, and displays on life beneath the ocean waves form the core of 140 permanent exhibits at the Miami Museum of Science and Space Transit Planetarium. The Collections Gallery holds geological specimens, fossilised sharks' teeth, mounted insects, spiders and butterflies, and several examples of how not to enjoy nature, such as an ashtray mounted on four Cayman heads. Outside in the Wildlife Center are a walk-through aviary, tortoises, eagles, and an 11-foot python. An enormous globe marks the entrance to the adjacent Planetarium, which stages astronomy shows and laser extravaganzas.

Temporary thrills Many of the museum's most memorable exhibitions have been temporary installations, usually lasting several months. An affiliation with the Smithsonian Institution in Washington, D.C. brings many outstanding traveling shows. One such was Expeditions, which recounted the scientific exploration of the cultures of Latin American and the Caribbean. Others may complement the programs of the museum's wildlife center, such as Hunters of the Sky, which focused on birds of prey. Meanwhile, Sharks! Fact or Fantasy examined the myths and realities of these feared creatures: another exhibit had moving life-sized models of dinosaurs.

HIGHLIGHTS

- Snakes
- Giant tortoises
- Aviary
- Collections Gallery
- Planetarium
- Everglades diorama
- American crocodile
- Turkey vultures
- Lizards
- The Missing Link

INFORMATION

- ✚ Off map
- ✉ 3280 S. Miami Avenue
- ☎ 305/854-4247
- 🕐 Daily 10–6
- 🚇 Vizcaya
- 🚌 48
- ♿ Very good
- 💲 Moderate
- ↔ Barnacle State Historic Site (➤ 33), Plymouth Congregational Church (➤ 32), Vizcaya Museum and Gardens (➤ 36)

Top: An albino python
Below: Museum globe

13

VIZCAYA MUSEUM AND GARDENS

No Miami home has ever been grander than Vizcaya, which was built for a rich industrialist who thought nothing of spending $15 million to create a pseudo-Italian villa amid the jungle-like landscapes of 1916 Miami.

HIGHLIGHTS

- Music Room
- Renaissance Hall
- Tea Room
- Breakfast Room
- Adams Library
- Banquet Hall
- Deering Bedroom
- Deering Bath
- Great Stone Barge
- Gardens

INFORMATION

- ✚ Off map
- ✉ 3251 S. Miami Avenue
- ☎ 305/250-9133
- 🕐 Daily 9:30–5
- 🍴 Café
- 🚇 Vizcaya
- 🚌 48
- ♿ Good
- 💵 Moderate
- ↔ Barnacle State Historic Site (➤ 33), Museum of Science (➤ 35), Plymouth Congregational Church (➤ 32)

The building Wealthy James Deering developed a liking for winter in Florida and commissioned architect F. Burral Hoffman, Jr., and artistic supervisor Paul Chalfin to create a palatial home on forest-covered land purchased from Miami settler William Brickell in 1912. At a time when Miami's population numbered 10,000, 1,000 people worked on the building of Vizcaya, which was intended to resemble an Italian villa that had been lived in for 400 years. After its completion, a small army stayed on as servants, gardeners, and handymen. Deering himself took up residence on Christmas Day 1916. Rooms were designed in a mixture of styles, and furnishings reflected the fashions of different eras. Nonetheless, Vizcaya's diverse strands—Italian Renaissance, baroque, rococo, or neoclassical—come together with surprising cohesion.

The rooms Deering's dinner guests were expected to arrive by gondola, navigating the Venetian-style Great Stone Barge, which serves as a breakwater, and entering Vizcaya from Biscayne Bay. Today's visitors enter from the other side of the airy courtyard, greeted by a statue of Bacchus that marks the starting point of free guided tours. These are essential in understanding a house whose 34 rooms each hold decorative treasures and anecdotal interest, alongside innovations in domestic architecture such as elevators, a swimming pool, and a bowling alley. Allow ample time to enjoy the 10-acre Italian and French formal gardens.

14

HISTORICAL MUSEUM

Spanning indigenous cultures, the Spanish era, and the rise of Miami itself, this museum covers the region's past with absorbing exhibits and a wealth of historical objects, as well as giving a useful outline of the area's ecology.

Beginnings Portrayals of the natural environment flow neatly into exhibits on the lives and lifestyles of the indigenous inhabitants of the area, chiefly the Tequesta people. Numerous artifacts from galleons and early settlements detail the arrival of the Spanish, Florida's first Europeans, whose presence led to the eventual disappearance of the Tequesta.

Seminole Indians Not until the 19th century did European settlement gain a lasting foothold in southern Florida as Key West emerged as a center for salvaging and cigar production, a period recalled at the museum by reconstructed buildings. Meanwhile, the Seminole people—Creek Indians who traveled south from Georgia during the 1700s and were forced into the Everglades by the 19th-century U.S.–Seminole Wars—are acknowledged with numerous everyday items, including clothing and a chickee hut.

Miami's settlement Evocative photographs capture the Miami and Coconut Grove of the 1890s, and the meeting of the 350 residents that formed Miami into a city in 1896. The museum also documents the arrival of the railroad, the 1920s land boom, and the growth of tourism, along with the segregation of earlier times, illustrated by the streetcar with separate seating areas for white and black travelers. Periodical temporary exhibitions cover more recent events.

HIGHLIGHTS

- Seminole patchwork jacket
- 1925 Miami streetcar
- 16th-century Spanish swivel gun
- Maps of the New World
- Photographs of pioneer life
- Art-deco ornaments
- 16th-century Spanish host press
- Prohibition exhibits

INFORMATION

- F8
- Metro-Dade Cultural Center, 101 W. Flagler Street
- 305/375-1492
- Mon–Wed, Fri, Sat 10–5; Thu 10–9; Sun noon–5
- Government Center
- All serving Downtown Miami
- Good
- Inexpensive
- Federal Courthouse (➤ 38), Metro-Dade Cultural Center (➤ 58), Metromover (➤ 60), Miami Art Museum of Dade County (➤ 54)

Top: Miami streetcar exhibit

15

FEDERAL COURTHOUSE

Miami's adjoining federal courthouses reflect the increasing importance of the city while showcasing some of its most attractive architecture. A controversial mural depicts the city's development.

The old The late 1920s found expanding Miami in need of a new main post office. Architect Phineas Paist and designer Denman Fink, both renowned for their work in Coral Gables, were selected to create a combined post office, courthouse, and federal office building. Opened in 1933, the building has a stately facade of Corinthian columns separating tall, arched windows. Inside is the main corridor, with a patterned marble floor beneath a vaulted ceiling and many eye-catching brass fittings. On the second floor, the Central Courtroom holds Denman Fink's majestic mural *Law Guides Florida Progress*, intended to depict Miami's development from savage backwater to enlightened modern city unfairly portraying the Seminole people as barbarians.

The new Porticoes on the west side of the courthouse lead into a shady Mediterranean-style courtyard, a good place to contemplate the building's form and to appreciate the sharp contrast in style provided by the predominantly concrete and glass New Courthouse, opened in 1983 and adjoining its predecessor. The first high-profile trial held in the curving, acoustically sensitive courtrooms inside the 11-story towers of the New Courthouse was the 1992 drug-trafficking trial of Panama's General Manuel Noriega. Global attention again focused on the building in 1999 during the legal battle over custody of Elian Gonzalez, and in the following year's dispute over Florida votes cast in the presidential election.

THE ATLANTIS

Said to have been first sketched on a napkin in a local Cuban restaurant, the Atlantis—featured in TV's Miami Vice—is an ebullient representative of the modern city's creative energy.

A significant gap Close to Downtown and next to Biscayne Bay, Brickell Avenue is a prime address, lined by stylish office towers and even more stylish condominiums. No building on Brickell Avenue, however, can compare with the innovative Atlantis, a condominium created by the local architectural firm Arquitectonica in 1978. Four yellow balconies and a bold red triangle on one end of the roof interrupt the gleaming reflective glass of the north facade. Yet the most daring and dramatic feature is simply a gap, a cutaway square section through the twelfth floor where a palm tree and a jacuzzi occupy a yellow-walled communal "sky patio," which is accessed by a red spiral staircase.

Close up The "missing" cube from the center of the building can be seen on the ground on the south side, housing a squash court and exercise room for residents. Meanwhile, the southern facade's light-gray cantilevered balconies are concealed within a monumental blue masonry grid, aesthetically thrilling and providing essential shade. From the side you can see how narrow the building is. Though 300 feet long and 20 stories high, the Atlantis is only 37 feet wide, with just six apartments on each floor. Those facing Biscayne Bay benefit from the Atlantis's curving eastern end, providing living rooms with a 180-degree water view.

DID YOU KNOW?

- Architects: Arquitectonica
- Developer: Solomon Luger & Samuel Greenberg
- Designed: 1978
- Completed: 1982
- Cost: $11.5 million
- Units: 96
- Stories: 20
- Underground car parking spaces: 200
- Size of each side of "missing" cube: 37 feet

INFORMATION

- E10
- 2025 Brickell Avenue
- Private residences; view from street only
- 5th Street
- 24, 48

Stylish interiors

FREEDOM TOWER

INFORMATION

- ✚ F7
- ✉ 600 Biscayne Boulevard
- ◷ View from street only
- ⌂ Freedom Tower
- ▭ 3, 16, 48, 95, C, S
- ⬌ Federal Courthouse (➤ 38), Historical Museum of Southern Florida (➤ 37), Metro-Dade Cultural Center (➤ 58), Metromover (➤ 60), Miami Art Museum of Dade County (➤ 54)

In a city devoted to the future and in a downtown area largely bereft of historic structures, the Freedom Tower remains an admired, if neglected, survivor, and for many Miami Cubans is a symbol of the new life they began in the city.

Repeated vacancies Completed in 1925, the Freedom Tower was originally named the Daily News Tower and was home to a leading local newspaper. It was one of architects Schultze & Weaver's two Miami structures inspired by the Giralda bell tower in Seville, Spain (the other being the tower of the Biltmore Hotel ➤ 26). The departure of the newspaper left the impressive structure empty until 1962, when the U.S. Government made it a processing center for Cuban refugees, some 230,000 of whom arrived on the "freedom flights" from Havana that continued until 1974. The curtailment of the flights signaled another period of vacancy for the tower. It remains closed despite a $25-million renovation in the late 1980s carried out with the intention of turning it into high-class offices topped by a city-view restaurant (an ill-fated undertaking, as it transpired).

At a distance, up close A three-story base surmounted by a 12-story tower rising to a two-story cupola, the building is better enjoyed from a distance, at its best on sunny days. Inside are multicolored handmade ceramic tiles, oak doors, and Oriental carpets, though you can't see them until the tower is once again open to the public. Because of its symbolic significance for Miami's Cuban population, there are often protests and other gatherings outside. Plans are underway to open the first floor as a museum of Cubans in Miami.

AMERICAN POLICE HALL OF FAME

The 11,000 exhibits at the American Police Hall of Fame and Museum paint a complete picture of police work in the United States, concentrating on high-profile gangsters as well as the routine work that underpins daily procedures.

Master criminals The presentation of police work as a struggle between the forces of good and evil is unrelenting. Nonetheless, there is much to pore over and enjoy. Several areas are assigned to history's notorious villains, including John Dillinger, who committed a series of armed bank robberies beginning in the late 1920s and was famously described as Public Enemy Number One before the mysterious lady-in-red betrayed him. A former Miami resident and leading gangster of the Prohibition era, Al Capone, is remembered by his hat, his personal telephone, and a pictorial spread on the St. Valentine's Day Massacre of 1929, in which Capone eliminated his rivals to take control of the Chicago underworld.

Crime and punishment Alongside the exhibits of police uniforms and helmets from around the world are oddities such as a Gestapo dagger and the rifle that belonged to Lee Harvey Oswald, alleged killer of John Kennedy, as well as unnerving items such as an electric chair and a gas chamber. Check out the FBI's display of the current Ten Most Wanted Men (some of whom may be women), or attempt to solve the re-created crime scene who-dunnit. A first floor memorial records the names of U.S. police officers slain on duty since 1960.

HIGHLIGHTS

- Dillinger exhibit
- Electric chair
- Gas chamber
- Capone exhibit
- Homemade weapons
- Drugs exhibit
- Satanism exhibit
- Officers' Memorial

INFORMATION

- ✚ F3
- ✉ 3801 Biscayne Boulevard
- ☎ 305/573-0070
- ⏰ Daily 10–5:30
- 🚌 3, 16, 62, J, T
- ♿ Excellent
- 🎫 Inexpensive

Robocop exhibit

19

ANCIENT SPANISH MONASTERY

HIGHLIGHTS

- The Chapel
- Baptismal font
- Hymnarium
- Pope Urban VII's cabinet
- 16th-century cabinet
- 12th-century *Christ the King* statue
- Telescopic windows above altar
- Iron gate
- Garden walk
- The corbels

INFORMATION

- ✚ Off map
- ✉ 16711 W. Dixie Highway
- ☎ 305/945-1462
- 🕐 Mon–Sat 10–4; Sun 1:30–5:30
- 🚌 3, E, H, V
- ♿ Good
- 🎟 Inexpensive

Miami's least likely building is a 12th-century monastery from Segovia, Spain. Imported piece by piece by the hugely rich William Randolph Hearst in 1925, it didn't arrive in Miami until nearly 30 years later.

Transit troubles   Having acquired a fortune through his vast newspaper empire, Hearst traveled Europe in the 1920s buying whatever caught his eye. One such item was an abandoned Cistercian monastery. Hearst paid $500,000 for the cloisters and outbuildings, and had them dismantled and packed into 11,000 numbered crates for shipment to the United States. Because of an outbreak of cattle disease in Spain, U.S. authorities opened the crates and removed and burned the straw used to pack the stones. The monastery was still in storage in New York when the Depression hit, eroding Hearst's wealth; Federal tax demands forced him to sell many of his assets.

A new home   In 1952, a year after Hearst's death, the monastery was purchased by two entrepreneurs who viewed it as a potential Florida tourist attraction. When the crates arrived in Miami, it was discovered that they had been incorrectly repacked in New York so rebuilding proceeded by trial and error (and took 19 months). Today's structure is charming but slightly higgledy-piggledy, with several modern enhancements such as the Cuban-tiled floor. The monastery reacquired a religious function in 1964 when it was bought by the Episcopal Church. It is now a place of worship and a photogenic wedding venue. A small museum recalls the monastery's past, and has Spanish historical items.

20

CAPE FLORIDA STATE RECREATION AREA

Though severely damaged by Hurricane Andrew, Cape Florida State Recreation Area, at the tip of Key Biscayne, is one of the most appealing natural areas in Miami. It is overlooked by the 19th–century Cape Florida lighthouse.

The park Rare plants and thick belts of trees made up the heart of Bill Baggs Cape Florida State Recreation Area until 1992, when Hurricane Andrew uprooted the trees and salt water decimated the plants. Thanks to a major replanting effort in the mid-1990s, new greenery is steadily overwhelming the natural devastation. The white sandy beach that frames the 406-acre park, popular on weekends, is virtually deserted during the week. Woodland paths and a beachside boardwalk make cycling or strolling the park easy, and bring plenty of docile wildlife such as racoons and squirrels into view.

The lighthouse Cape Florida is one of the oldest named places in the United States, having been chronicled by Juan Ponce de León in 1513. Decommissioned in 1978, the current Cape Florida lighthouse is a taller brick reconstruction of an 1825 original. The structure has a dramatic history; its assistant keeper was slain in 1836 during the Second Seminole War, and its beacon extinguished by Confederate forces in an attempt to disrupt Union shipping during the Civil War. Lighthouse and parkland were purchased by the state for preservation in 1966. The lighthouse's living quarters have been reconstructed and an absorbing ranger-led tour reveals much about the lighthouse itself and life in 19th-century southern Florida. Its beacon was relit to mark Miami's centennial celebrations in 1996.

Above: Park squirrel
Top: Cape Florida lighthouse

DID YOU KNOW?

- Area: 406 acres
- Beach length: 1 mile
- Lighthouse's original height: 65 feet
- Lighthouse's current height: 95 feet

INFORMATION

- ✚ Off map
- ✉ 1200 S. Crandon Boulevard
- ☎ 305/361-5811
- 🕐 Daily 8–sunset
- 🚌 B
- ♿ Good
- 💲 Inexpensive
- ↔ Crandon Park (► 52), Miami Seaquarium (► 55), Virginia Key Beach (► 53)

21

HOLOCAUST MEMORIAL

DID YOU KNOW?

- Memorial idea suggested: 1984
- Architect and sculptor: Kenneth Treister
- Official opening: 1990
- Diameter of lily pond: 200 feet

INFORMATION

- ✚ M5
- ✉ 1933–45 Meridian Avenue
- ☎ 305/538-1663
- 🕐 Daily 9–9
- 🚌 A, G, K
- ♿ Good
- 💷 Free
- ↔ Bass Museum of Art (➤ 47), Jewish Museum of Florida (➤ 46), South Florida Art Center (➤ 60), The Wolfsonian (➤ 45)

Miami has a substantial Jewish community and one of the world's largest populations of Holocaust survivors. So it is fitting that a major memorial to the six million victims of Nazi genocide should stand here.

Horror Visitors pass first through the Arbor of History, which outlines the story of the Jewish presence in Europe and the rise of Nazism. Horrifying photographs recall 1938's *Kristallnacht* and the cattle cars into which Nazi victims were packed for the journey to concentration camps. By far the most affecting section of the memorial is reached through the short tunnel named the Lonely Path, lined with the names of the most infamous concentration camps—the somber tunnel gradually diminishes in size to suggest the camps' role in diminishing the individual. Emerging from the tunnel, you are confronted by Kenneth Treister's 42-feet-high bronze statue of an arm and hand—visible from the street and reaching in anguish for the sky—and by nearly 100 tormented human figures.

Time for reflection Many of the sculptured figures are seeking to climb the raised arm to an open hand, representing freedom; some are scattered around the foreground. You have no choice but to walk among them—and when you do, you are crowded by indescribable suffering. The concluding section of the memorial holds the Memorial Wall, etched with thousands of Holocaust victims' names. The Reflective Pool, filled with oversized lilies, is a tranquil epilogue to the heart-wrenching story of atrocities and genocide, and gives you the chance to contemplate the tragic things you have seen.

THE WOLFSONIAN

You might see an Eiffel Tower–shaped teapot. Or maybe a machine for testing the chewing ability of the average mouth. Whatever you encounter at the hard-to-define Wolfsonian, it's sure to be very intriguing.

The background A member of a long-prominent Miami family, known for its entertainment and media empire, who inherited a fortune in the late 1980s, Mitchell Wolfson, Jr., was—and continues to be—an avid collector with a special passion for art and design items of between 1885 and 1945. Confronted by high storage costs for his collection of more than 70,000 pieces, Wolfson simply bought the warehouse, a 1927 architectural landmark and the current site of the Wolfsonian. Refusing to be labeled a museum or institution, the Wolfsonian houses a design research center, opened in 1993, and public galleries, opened in 1995, amid the art-deco buildings of South Beach. The Wolfsonian's white facade is near-windowless so your attention is drawn to the intricate Spanish baroque bas-reliefs, which subtly pull you toward the entrance.

The exhibitions Many of the interior fittings are drawn from the collection, and none is more stunning than the green and gold terra-cotta facade of a 1920s Pennsylvania movie theater that rises in the lobby. Inside, elevated walkways connect the galleries and give views across the South Beach rooftops. Exhibitions usually last several months and feature anything from Italian Futurist posters to Moderne cocktail shakers. Rather than simply presenting the objects or artworks, the exhibitions aim to highlight their cultural and technological context, making for stimulating viewing.

DID YOU KNOW?

- Exhibition area: 12,000sq feet
- Holdings: 70,000
- Decorative art objects: 9,000
- Posters, paintings, drawings, and prints: 12,500
- Research library: 36,000 items

INFORMATION

- M7
- 1001 Washington Avenue
- 305/531-1001
- Mon, Wed, Fri, Sat 10–6; Thu 10–9; Sun noon–5
- C, H, K, W
- Excellent
- Inexpensive; free Thu 6–9
- Bass Museum of Art (➤ 47), Holocaust Memorial (➤ 44), Jewish Museum of Florida (➤ 46), South Florida Art Center (➤ 60)

The Wolfsonian's water fountain

23

JEWISH MUSEUM OF FLORIDA

DID YOU KNOW?

A growing community

- 1763: As Florida becomes a British possession, Jews are permitted to live openly
- 1845: As Florida joins the Union and becomes a state, its first senator, David Yulee, is Jewish and is also the first Jewish senator in the country
- 1857: Jewish cemetery established in Jacksonville
- 1943: Mitchell Wolfson, Jr., becomes first Jewish mayor of Miami Beach
- 1959: First of 10,000 Cuban Jews arrive in Miami, escaping the Castro regime

INFORMATION

- ✚ M8
- ✉ 301 Washington Avenue
- ☎ 305/672-5044
- 🕐 Tue–Sun 10–5. Closed Mon and Jewish holidays
- ▣ C, H, K
- ♿ Few
- 💲 Inexpensive
- ↔ Bass Museum of Art (▶ 47), Holocaust Memorial (▶ 44), South Florida Art Center (▶ 60), The Wolfsonian (▶ 45)

Occupying an historic building and drawing attention to an important chapter in local history, the Sanford L. Ziff Jewish Museum of Florida offers illuminating insights into the history of Florida's Jewish community.

The exhibits A brief history of Jewish settlement throughout the world greets you as you enter the museum, setting the tone for myriad exhibits. It is thought that some Jews who had converted to Christianity during the Inquisition, arrived with the 16th-century Spanish landings, but Florida's first Jewish settlers arrived in Pensacola in 1763. Not until the inter-war years did the Miami Jewish community develop a prominent profile. The subsequent steady growth of the community is recorded here with everyday items, religious artifacts, and photographs. It is a sobering thought to recall the discrimination Jews faced despite their huge numbers. For many years local laws dictated that they were not allowed to live north of 5th Street and tourist hotels advertised with the slogan "always a view, never a Jew."

The building Completed in 1936 for the first Jewish congregation in Miami Beach, the handsome museum building was originally an Orthodox synagogue. Its architect, Henry Hohauser, was among the leading lights of the local art-deco style, with some 300 buildings to the firm's credit. As the congregation declined, so too did the synagogue, which was also battered by Hurricane Andrew in 1992. Now restored, it has pews for meetings and 77 stained-glass windows, including one in memory of the notorious gangster Meyer Lansky. The upper levels, originally reserved for women, are now administrative offices.

Top: Stained-glass window detail

BASS MUSEUM OF ART

One of the area's earliest art-deco buildings, the Bass Museum of Art houses a near-priceless collection of paintings, sculpture, and tapestries from European masters, and stages acclaimed temporary shows.

Architecture Fronted by gardens laid out in the 1920s, the Bass Museum of Art began life as a library that, in 1930, became the first public building in Miami designed with space for exhibiting fine art. The architect gave Mayan features to the sturdy-looking structure of keystone, a type of coral rock from the Florida Keys, and had the main entrance decorated by bas-reliefs and wrought-iron sidelights. In the 1960s, the library became the Bass Museum of Art, after a new larger library was built and the multi-million-dollar art collection of John and Johanna Bass was donated. Renowned architect Arata Isozaki is behind the present $8 million expansion, which eventually adds more exhibition space and will eventually create a culture park reaching to the ocean.

Art The Basses had amassed some 500 European pieces, among them 167 paintings by artists as diverse as Peter Paul Rubens and Sir Thomas Lawrence, important 16th- and 17th-century textiles, and sculpture from the 15th to the 17th centuries. These items form the core of the museum's permanent collection; Cornelis van Haarlem's *Crucifixion Triptych* and Ferdinand Bol's *Venus and Adonis* are particularly impressive. Altogether grander, however, are a pair of immense 19th-century French-Belgian tapestries, *The Start of the Hunt* and *The Return from the Hunt*. Displayed nearby, *The Tournament*, of the 16th-century Flemish School, is among the most important tapestries on view in the United States.

HIGHLIGHTS

- *The Tournament*, Flemish School
- *Crucifixion Triptych*, Van Haarlem

INFORMATION

- ✚ M5
- ✉ 2121 Park Avenue
- ☎ 305/673-7530
- ◷ Tue–Sat 10–5; Sun 1–5; 2nd and 4th Wed of month 1–9
- 🚇 C, F/M, G, H, L, S
- ♿ Good
- 🍴 Inexpensive
- ↔ South Florida Art Center (➤ 60), The Wolfsonian (➤ 45)

Top: The Flight of Lot and His Family from Sodom, *Peter Paul Rubens*
Below: Egyptian inner sarcophagus

47

25

FONTAINEBLEAU HOTEL

A procession of high-rise hotels has filled the central section of Miami Beach since the 1950s, but none can match the character or the architectural audacity of the Fontainebleau, once the last word in luxury and still a sight to behold.

Creation Built on the site of tire mogul Harvey Firestone's mansion, the Fontainebleau (pronounced "Fountain Blue") opened its doors in 1954, when Miami Beach was the nation's premier vacation destination. Celebrities such as Bob Hope, Elvis Presley, and Judy Garland stayed and entertained, while a long list of movies were shot here, including the whole of Jerry Lewis's 1960 *The Bell Boy*. Designed by architect Morris Lapidus in a daring sweeping curve, the hotel originally had 550 rooms, 230 yards of beachfront, a raised swimming pool with an ocean view, and antique-packed interiors based on a French theme. The main lobby covered 17,000sq feet, while the lower lobby had a post office, health clinic, a stockbrokers' office, and a coffee shop. The dance floor of the 800-seat supper club is hydraulically controlled.

Continuation As vacation patterns changed, so too, did the Fontainebleau. By the late 1970s, the hotel was being managed by the Hilton group, which revamped it inside and out. Money was lavished on refurbishing guest rooms and other areas, and the pool area was transformed by the addition of a half-acre grotto, with artificial waterfalls, a palm-tree-lined island, and three temperature-controlled jacuzzis. In 1985, muralist Richard Haas was commissioned to design the striking trompe l'oeil that covers more than a quarter-acre of the hotel's south wall, giving a realistic view of the hotel through an illusory triumphal arch.

MIAMI's
best

49

NEIGHBORHOODS

Café Sci Sci on Coconut Grove

New ethnic neighborhoods

Miami has long been a place of refuge for those in need from Latin America and the Caribbean. Around 54th Street and Miami Avenue is Little Haiti, created by an influx of Haitians in the late 1970s. About the same time, around 75,000 Nicaraguans settled in Sweetwater, on Miami's western edge, now described as Little Managua.

COCONUT GROVE
A hundred years ago, Coconut Grove was a separate and more successful settlement than Miami, and it still has the sense of being aloof from the city that engulfs it. Madonna and Sylvester Stallone are two of the many celebrities who have bought homes here, either palatial bayside dwellings or million-dollar condominiums with stunning views. Local activity focuses on the trendy stores, chic restaurants, and many bars around the junction of Main Highway and McFarlane Road, and on the events that take place in nearby Peacock Park.
➕ Off map 🚇 Coconut Grove 🚌 42, 48, 65

CORAL GABLES
Described with some justification as "the City Beautiful" by developer George Merrick in the 1920s, Coral Gables is a quiet but commercially vibrant area characterized by the Mediterranean-style architecture and Spanish street names. Elegant stores line the landscaped Miracle Mile, and many coral-rock homes stand on tree-edged residential streets.
➕ Off map 🚌 24, 37, 40, 42, 56, J

DOWNTOWN
With its local and Federal government building, and its many high-rise offices, Downtown is an administrative and business center largely deserted at

night. By day, many Miamians do their shopping here in countless mini-malls, as street vendors proffer refreshing fruit drinks and sidewalk snack bars dispense *café Cubano* and mighty Cuban sandwiches.

✛ E/F/G 7/8 🚇 Government Center 🚌 All serving Downtown

KEY BISCAYNE

Linked to the mainland by the soaring Rickenbacker Causeway, Key Biscayne is a pristine island community with secluded homes and a handful of luxury hotels in a landscape dominated by Australian pines and beaches fringed by coconut palms. Though many trees succumbed to Hurricane Andrew in 1992, Key Biscayne still provides an escape from urban Miami, its residential mid-section wedged between Crandon Park Beach (► 52) and the Cape Florida State Recreation Area (► 43).

✛ Off map 🚌 B

The Electrowave

Electrically-powered shuttle buses (the Electrowave) operate on Washington Avenue in South Beach between 5th and 17th streets. The fare is 25c.

LITTLE HAVANA

Earning its name following a mass Cuban influx into Miami during the early 1960s, Little Havana was where most newly arrived Cubans settled. The local section of S.W. 8th Street is the main thoroughfare, better known throughout Miami as *Calle Ocho*. The scene of a huge festival each March, it is also the site of innumerable Cuban businesses and markers to heroes of the Caribbean island. Increasingly affluent and influential in Miami life, many Cubans have left Little Havana, and the area is becoming populated by refugees from Central America.

✛ C/D 8/9 🚌 8, 12, 17, 27

SOUTH BEACH

The site of Miami Beach's celebrated Art Deco District, South Beach is among the most fashion-conscious places in the United States. Since the 1980s, its beautifully restored buildings dating from the 1920s and 1930s have been patrolled by legions of fashion models and would-be fashion models, creating a sense of glamour and excitement amid pastel colors intensified by the subtropical sunshine. By day, music videos are shot in the street; after dark the bars and flamboyant nightclubs are jumping all night long.

✛ L/M/N 5/6/7/8/9 🚌 C, H, K, F/M, S

51

BEACHES & PARKS

See Top 25 Sights for
**CAPE FLORIDA STATE
RECREATION AREA (➤ 43)**

Little Havana parks

In the heart of Little Havana, Máximo Gómez Park (✚ C9 ✉ S.W. 8th Street and S.W. 14th Avenue 🚌 8, 12), finds mostly ageing Cuban men poised for hours over games of dominoes, pausing only to denounce Fidel Castro. On Little Havana's eastern edge, José Martí Park (✚ E8 ✉ 351 S.W. 4th Street), named after the Cuban writer and independence campaigner, provides a much-needed local recreation space.

Beach volleyball

BAYFRONT PARK
Created in the 1920s and greatly improved by a $30-million reshaping in the 1980s, landscaped Bayfront Park is fringed by blue waters and makes an enticing rest spot Downtown (➤ 50), near Bayside Marketplace (➤ 70). The park's amphitheater is regularly used for concerts.
✚ F/G 7/8 ✉ Off Biscayne Boulevard 🚇 Bayfront Park 🚌 3, 16, 48, 95, C, S

CRANDON PARK
A 3-mile beach shaded by coconut palms makes Crandon Park one of Miami's most popular weekend spots for sunbathing, swimming, and beach barbecues: fire rings are provided.
✚ Off map ✉ 4000 Crandon Boulevard, Key Biscayne 🚌 B

FIRST STREET BEACH
One of the few Miami beaches suitable for surfing, 1st Street Beach attracts plenty of board-wielding wave riders; adjacent are a smattering of loud and lively restaurants and bars.
✚ M8 ✉ East end of 1st Street 🚌 H, W

HAULOVER PARK
Haulover Park's raw expanse of grass, sea oats, and sand dunes provides a brief break in the wall of ocean-view condominiums lining central Miami Beach. Beyond there lies a mile-long beach that welcomes nudists.
✚ Off map ✉ 10800 Collins Avenue 🚌 H, K, S, T

LUMMUS PARK
With the ocean on one side and art-deco buildings on the other, this park with a beach is in the heart of fashionable South Beach; there's no better place for catching some rays and taking in the scene.
✚ M6/7 ✉ 10 Ocean Drive 🚌 C, G, H, W

MATHESON HAMMOCK PARK
A wonderful slice of natural southern Florida, Matheson Hammock Park comprises many acres of trees and coastal vegetation linked by shady pathways and culminating in a stretch of sand that, in 1930, became Miami's first public beach.
✚ Off map ✉ 9610 Old Cutler Road, Coral Gables 🚌 65

PEACOCK PARK

Named after a prominent Coconut Grove pioneer family and set on the site of southern Florida's first hotel, Peacock Park is a slender, sloping pocket of green with a baseball field and the Chamber of Commerce building. You'll often find special events on weekends.

✚ Off map ✉ 2820 McFarlane Road, Coconut Grove 🚇 Coconut Grove 🚌 42, 48, 65

RICKENBACKER PARK

Accessed from the western end of Rickenbacker Causeway, this modest park sits on Hobie Island. The beach is small, but the brisk breezes make it the most popular place in Miami to windsurf. Equipment can be rented on the spot.

✚ Off map 🚌 48

SOUTH POINTE PARK

Comprising 17 acres at the southernmost tip of South Beach, South Pointe Park has palm trees, winding pathways, and benches with a view of immense cruise ships as they glide in and out of port.

✚ M8/9 ✉ South of 1st Street 🚌 H, W

VIRGINIA KEY BEACH

A neighbor to Key Biscayne and similarly cloaked in Australian pines, Virginia Key has no residents and few visitors—except those who thread through its vegetation to enjoy secluded sunbathing on this fine-sand beach.

✚ Off map ✉ Rickenbacker Causeway 🚌 8

Amelia Earhart Park

Anyone whose passions include aviation and unsolved mysteries, might care to pay their respects at Amelia Earhart Park, named after the aviator whose fatal last flight took off from Miami. A good outing for kids, the park has playgrounds, fish-filled lakes with explorable islands and beaches, picnic facilities, and a down-home-style farm with animals to pet, pony rides, and demonstrations of old-time skills by blacksmiths and others.

✉ 401 E. 65th Street, Hialeah ☎ 305/685-8389 🚌 37 ♿ Good 🕐 Moderate

Miami Beach

MUSEUMS & ATTRACTIONS

More art

To check the pulse of the Miami art scene, visit the South Florida Art Center (► 60), which not only provides studio space for some of the region's most exciting visual artists and mounts regular exhibitions, but also played a major role in the revitalization of South Beach. Contained within three art-deco buildings, the center's 52 studios are open daily to the public.

CUBAN MUSEUM OF THE AMERICAS

With its temporary exhibitions displaying the works of Cuban artists living outside Cuba, this museum has at times generated controversy among expatriate Cubans for showing pieces by artists allegedly sympathetic to the revolution.

➕ D9 ✉ 1300 S.W. 12th Avenue ☎ 305/529-5400 ⏱ Usually weekends only by appointment 🚌 8, 12 ♿ Good 💲 Donation

FRUIT & SPICE PARK

Twenty acres of exotic vegetation with more than 500 species of fruit, herb, spice, and nut.

➕ Off map ✉ 24801 S.W. 187th Avenue ☎ 305/247-5727
⏱ Daily 10–5 ♿ Good 💲 Inexpensive

Lowe Art Gallery exhibit

GOLD COAST RAILROAD MUSEUM

The Gold Coast Railroad Museum, next to the Metrozoo, displays relics from the halcyon days of U.S. train travel, including the only custom-built Presidential Pullman car. It was made famous in President Harry S. Truman's 1948 reelection campaign.

➕ Off map ✉ 12450 S.W. 152nd Street
☎ 305/253-0063 ⏱ Daily 11–4 🚌 Zoo Express, from Dadeland North ♿ Good
💲 Inexpensive

MIAMI ART MUSEUM OF DADE COUNTY

Well-designed galleries with excellent and diverse exhibitions of modern and contemporary art from around the world.

➕ F8 ✉ Metro-Dade Cultural Center, 101 W. Flagler Street ☎ 305/375-1700
⏱ Tue, Wed, Fri 10–5; 3rd Thu of month 10–9; Sat, Sun

noon–5 🏛 Government Center 🚌 Any serving Downtown ♿ Good
💵 Inexpensive

MIAMI SEAQUARIUM
Killer whales and dolphins are among the stars of the
show that displays sea mammals' learning abilities
and skills. Other underwater creatures are displayed
in pools.
➕ Off map ✉ 4400 Rickenbacker Causeway ☎ 305/361-5705
🕐 Daily 9:30–6 🍴 Snack bars 🚇 B ♿ Good 💵 Moderate

MONKEY JUNGLE
Unrestricted by cages, protected primates from
Asia and South America roam the tropical woodland
watched by humans confined to fenced-in
walkways. Also on display is a large collection of
southern Florida fossils.
➕ Off map ✉ 14805 S.W. 216th Street ☎ 305/235-1611
🕐 Daily 9:30–5 🍴 Snack bar ♿ Few 💵 Moderate

MUSEUM OF CONTEMPORARY ART
This out-of-the-way North Miami museum is a
generously sized showplace that mounts strong
temporary exhibitions and displays a permanent
collection that includes works by Roy Liechtenstein,
Jasper Johns, and Claes Oldenberg.
➕ Off map ✉ 770 N.E. 125th Street ☎ 305/893-6211
🕐 Tue–Sat 10–5; Sun noon–5 🚇 G ♿ Good 💵 Moderate

PARROT JUNGLE & GARDENS
Parrots, birds of prey, endangered primates, giant
tortoises, and alligators are among the residents,
while the gardens display tropical flora from banana
trees to bromeliads.
➕ Off map ✉ 11000 S.W. 57th Avenue (projected to move 2003 to
Watson Island, off MacArthur Causeway) ☎ 305/666-7834 🕐 Daily
9:30–6 🍴 Café ♿ Few 💵 Moderate

*Killer whale, Miami
Seaquarium*

Weeks Air Museum

Before Miami International
Airport, the diminutive Tamiami
Airport (✉ 14710 S.W. 128th
Street) was the city's major air
terminal. Now used by private
planes, it has one hangar devoted
to the Weeks Air Museum
(☎ 305/233-5197), a mass of
propellers, engine parts,
undercarriages, and complete
planes spanning the early days of
powered flight to World War II.

HISTORIC BUILDINGS

Coral Gables Congregational Church

Miami Beach Old City Hall

Complete with Corinthian columns, urn finials, compass windows, and a barrel-tiled roof, this nine-story building symbolized Miami Beach's recovery from the previous year's devastating hurricane. It was designed in 1927.

✉ 1130 Washington Avenue

ALFRED I. DUPONT BUILDING
The Alfred I. Dupont Building, completed in 1938, is a fine example of the Depression-era Moderne style, a classical composition whose restrained art-deco elements can be seen at their decorative best in the second-floor lobby.
✚ F8 ✉ 169 E. Flagler Street 🚇 Miami Avenue 🚌 All serving Downtown

COLONNADE BUILDING
Spanish colonial and baroque meet in this 1920s Coral Gables landmark, fronted by two-story columns and elaborately decorated entrances that rise to a 75-foot-high rotunda with a red-tile roof. It is home to the Florida National Bank.
✚ Off map ✉ 133–169 Coral Way, Coral Gables 🚌 24, 37, 40, 42, 56, J

CORAL GABLES CONGREGATIONAL CHURCH
Completed in 1924, this pretty church has a Mediterranean style that fits perfectly into the Coral Gables landscape; the 16th-century furniture inside is said to have been salvaged from shipwrecks. It plays host to many book readings and concerts.
✚ Off map ✉ 3010 De Soto Boulevard 🚌 42, J

DADE COUNTY COURTHOUSE
The terra-cotta-fronted, classically inspired Dade County Courthouse, culminating in a ziggurat peak, dates from 1926; with 27 stories, it easily became the tallest building in Florida at that time.
✚ F8 ✉ 73 W. Flagler Street 🚇 Miami Avenue 🚌 All serving Downtown

EDEN ROC HOTEL
One of mid-Miami Beach's architecturally flamboyant 1950s hotels, designed by Morris Lapidus. An immense faux ship's funnel hides its rooftop pipework.
✚ N 2/3 ✉ 4525 Collins Avenue 🚌 C, F/M, G, H, L, S

FORT DALLAS BARRACKS

Built of coral rock in 1849 by pioneer settler William English, this building was used as slave quarters until it became Fort Dallas Barracks, housing troops fighting in the Seminole Wars.

✚ E7 ✉ 404 N.W. 3rd Street
Ⓜ Government Center 🚌 77

GESU CHURCH

Serving Miami's oldest Catholic parish, established in 1896, the 1920s Gesu Church is richly decorated inside. Services are in English or Spanish.

✚ F7 ✉ 118 N.E. 2nd Street
Ⓜ College Bayside 🚌 Most serving Downtown

HIALEAH PARK RACETRACK

This immaculately landscaped racetrack opened in 1932. Its flock of 400 flamingos is descended from one brought from Cuba when the track was built.

✚ Off map ✉ 2200 E. 4th Avenue Ⓜ Hialeah 🚌 37, L

MIAMI BEACH POST OFFICE

Inside the rotunda that forms the centerpiece of the 1937 Miami Beach Post Office, a Moderne masterpiece, are wonderful bronze fixtures and three breathtaking murals.

✚ M6 ✉ 1300 Washington Avenue 🚌 C, H, K, W

MIAMI CITY HALL

Originally the base for Pan American Airways' seaplane service to Latin America, this graceful 1930s building in Coconut Grove became Miami City Hall in 1954.

✚ Off map ✉ 3500 Pan American Drive 🚌 42, 48

OPA-LOCKA CITY HALL

The climax of the unrestrained Arabesque architecture with which developer Glenn Curtiss created Opa-locka in the 1920s is City Hall, a white and pink riot of spires, domes, minarets, and parapets.

✚ Off map ✉ 777 Sharazad Boulevard 🚌 27, 32, E

Above: Horse-racing
Below: Casa Casuarina

Casa Casuarina

In 1992, fashion designer Gianni Versace bought the pseudo 16th-century Amsterdam Palace and, with $6 million, combined it with the building next door, to create Casa Casaurina (✉ 1116 Ocean Drive), one of the most attractive and distinctive private homes on Ocean Drive. The wrought-iron gates are now a popular photo stop, not for the house's architecture but for the fact that it was here in July 1997 that Versace was fatally gunned down.

57

MODERN BUILDINGS

See Top 25 Sights for
THE ATLANTIS (► 39)
FEDERAL COURTHOUSE (► 38)

Portofino Tower

Built in 1997 in the previously low-rise, low-rent area south of 5th Street, 44-story Portofino Tower generated much controversy when it went up and became the tallest building in South Beach; its luxury penthouse apartments are priced in the region of $3 million.
➕ M8 ✉ One South Pointe Drive 🚇 H, W

BRICKELL AVENUE BANKING DISTRICT
Miami's 1980s role as a financial center has left a row of gleaming high-rise bank offices lining this section of Brickell Avenue.
➕ F9 ✉ Brickell Avenue between 5th and 15th streets
🚇 Brickell/5th Street/8th Street 🚌 24, 48, 95

FIRST UNION FINANCIAL CENTER
Florida's tallest building, designed by Charles E. Bassett and Skidmore, Owings, and Merrill during the mid-1980s Downtown building boom, has 55 glass and steel stories.
➕ F7 ✉ 200 S. Biscayne Boulevard 🚇 1st Street 🚌 3, 16, 48, 95, C, S

GOVERNMENT CENTER
On the lower levels of this complex of city and county administrative offices, cleverly integrated walkways and escalators move people between public transportation terminals and through shops and a food plaza.
➕ F7 🚇 Government Center 🚌 All serving Downtown

INTERNATIONAL PLAZA
Ingeniously designed by I. M. Pei in the late 1980s, the 48-story former CenTrust Tower appears to be a cut-away cylinder. The tower is colorfully illuminated at night.
➕ F8 ✉ 100 S.E. 1st Street 🚇 Knight Center 🚌 All serving Downtown

METRO-DADE CULTURAL CENTER
Architect Philip Johnson devised this Mediterranean-style setting for the Historical Museum of Southern Florida (► 37), Miami Art Museum of Dade County (► 54), and the Miami-Dade Public Library in 1984.
➕ E/F 7/8 ✉ 101 W. Flagler Street 🚇 Government Center 🚌 All serving Downtown

Brickell Avenue

FOR KIDS

See Top 25 Sights for
CORAL CASTLE (▶ 25)
MIAMI METROZOO (▶ 24)
MUSEUM OF SCIENCE (▶ 35)
VENETIAN POOL (▶ 29)

BISCAYNE NATURE CENTER
Junior naturalists will enjoy the hands-on programs; marine exploration, beach and fossil reef walks, and coastal hammock hikes.
🏕 Off map ✉ Crandon Park, Key Biscayne ☎ 305/642-9600
🚇 South Miami 🚌 B

GAMEWORKS
An outpost of the Steven Spielberg-devised chain of indoor entertainment centers. State-of-the-art interactive games whisk kids into dinosaur attacks, intergalactic battles, drag racing, and jet skiing.
🏕 Off map ✉ Sunset Place (Suite 330), 5701 Sunset Drive
☎ 305/667-4263 or 800/777-4263 🚇 South Miami 🚌 57, 65, 72

GOLD COAST RAILROAD MUSEUM (▶ 54)
MIAMI SEAQUARIUM (▶ 55)

HOUSE OF TERROR
Ghoulishly attired staff and clever special effects chill, shock, and surprise in this spooky "haunted house."
🏕 Off map ✉ Streets of Mayfair, Grand Avenue, Coconut Grove
☎ 305/338-8892 🕐 Daily 4PM–11PM (closing hours may vary)
🚌 27, 42, 48 💳 Moderate

MONKEY JUNGLE (▶ 55)
PARROT JUNGLE & GARDENS (▶ 55)

IMAX THEATER AT SUNSET PLACE
Six-story-high images are accompanied by wrap-around sound. Some films are 3-D.
🏕 Off map ✉ Sunset Place (Suite 134), 5701 Sunset Drive ☎ 305/663-4629 🚇 South Miami 🚌 57, 65, 72

SCOTT RAKOW YOUTH CENTER
Supervised basketball and gym facilities, bowling alleys, and an ice-skating rink. Adults on Sundays only.
🏕 M4 ✉ 2700 Sheridan Avenue ☎ 305/673-7767 🚌 C, F/M, G, H, L, S

SKATE 2000
This shop sells in-line skates and offers free lessons.
🏕 M7 ✉ 1200 Ocean Drive ☎ 305/538-8282
🚌 C, H, W

Watersports
Biscayne Bay is an ideal spot for watersports. Sailboats of Key Biscayne (☎ 305/361-0328) offers sailing courses, and there are family scuba and snorkel tours from Biscayne National Park (▶ 20). Take to the mangrove-lined waterways of Miami Beach in a rented canoe from Haulover Park (☎ 305/947-1302, ▶ 52). At Cape Florida State Recreation Area (▶ 43) kids can rent hydrobikes and go swimming.

Parrot Jungle residents

WHAT'S FREE

Ermita de la Caridad

The conically shaped Ermita de la Caridad church (✉ 3609 S. Miami Avenue ☎ 305/854-2404) sits beside Biscayne Bay within walking distance of Vizcaya (► 36) but much less visited. The church serves a largely Cuban congregation: busts of José Martí and Padre Felix Valera face the bay—and Cuba—while inside, above the altar, an intricate mural depicts the history of the Catholic church in Cuba.

HIBISCUS, PALM, AND STAR ISLANDS

These three artificial islands within Biscayne Bay are entirely residential and decidedly wealthy. Although no homes are particularly spectacular, the list of former residents includes writer Damon Runyon, gangster Al Capone, and *Miami Vice* star Don Johnson.

✚ H/J/K 6/7/8 ✉ Off MacArthur Causeway 🚌 C, K, F/M, S

ICHIMURA MIAMI-JAPAN GARDEN

Japanese industrialist Kiyoshi Ichimura presented Miami with this landscaped acre in 1961, its walkways and dainty bridges reaching to the Hakkaku-Do, an octagonal building raised in the style of a Japanese Buddhist shrine.

✚ H6 ✉ Watson Island, off MacArthur Causeway ☎ 305/538-2121
🕐 Mon–Fri 8–3:30; Sat 10–4; Sun noon–4 🚌 C, K, F/M, S
♿ Good

METROMOVER

It may not quite be free, but for just 25¢ you can ride this single carriage train viewing the Downtown skyline from above, or in the case of the taller buildings, alongside, while moving at what seems like a snail's pace.

Metromover

✚ F7/8 ✉ Downtown
☎ 305/638-6700
🕐 6–midnight; best to use during daylight hours ♿ Good

SOUTH FLORIDA ART CENTER

Three historic, restored buildings on the pedestrianized Lincoln Road comprise the South Florida Art Center, providing working space for artists, art classes, and discussion groups, and displays of new work in four exhibition galleries.

✚ L6 ✉ 800, 810, 924 Lincoln Road ☎ 305/674-8278 🕐 Daily 11–11 🚌 K, F/M, S, W ♿ Few

MIAMI
where to...

NEW FUSION CUISINE

Prices

Expect to pay per person for a meal, excluding drink:

S	up to $15
SS	up to $35
SSS	more than $35

All the restaurants listed are open daily for lunch and dinner unless otherwise stated.

New Floridian cuisine

Food critics are excited about the innovative dishes created by Miami-based American chefs using the extraordinary range of produce from the Caribbean and Central America (Floribbean fare). These innovators conjure up exciting and picturesques dishes, featuring regional fish and exotic fruits, vegetables, and spices. Norman van Aken, Allan Susser, and Mark Militello are the chief exponents, imitated by increasing numbers of enthusiastic followers.

BALEEN ($$$)

At this glamorous restaurant on the water, Chef Robbin Haas is another Floribbean star. Sunday brunch is a must, and be sure to try the Asian bouillabaisse. Ask for a table outside.
Off map ✉ Grove Isle Resort, 4 Grove Isle Drive, Coconut Grove ☎ 305/858-8300 🚌 48

BLUE DOOR ($$$)

Creative, contemporary American cooking takes in tuna foie gras, open-faced raviolo served with rabbit, and Maine lobster in coconut milk broth.
M6 ✉ Delano Hotel, 1685 Collins Avenue ☎ 305/674-6400 🚌 C, G, F/M, H, L, S

CHEF ALLEN'S ($$$)

Allen Susser's artfully conceived cuisine is South Florida dining at its best. The open kitchen lets you watch the bustle as the kitchen turns out dishes like bay scallops with sweet potato ravioli and red wine vinegar.
Off map ✉ 19088 N.E. 29th Avenue (191st Street), N. Miami Beach ☎ 305/935-2900 🕐 Dinner only

MARK'S SOUTH BEACH ($$$)

Top-rated Florida chef Mark Militello constantly wows Miami's discerning diners. This is the latest of several city restaurants bearing his name and sets a blistering standard, with devilishly good food.
M7 ✉ Hotel Nash, 1120 Collins Avenue 🕐 Dinner only ☎ 305/604-9050 🚌 C, H, K, W

NEMO ($$–$$$)

Celebrity chef Michael Schwartz brings his Asian-inspired cooking to this see-and-be-seen art-deco building.
M8 ✉ 100 Collins Avenue ☎ 305/532-4550 🚌 H, W

NORMAN'S ($$$)

Norman Van Aken is regularly voted the best chef in the city. His New World dishes are complex but the exquisite flavors sing out loud and clear. Highly professional service. Worth the splurge.
Off map ✉ 21 Almeria Avenue, Coral Gables ☎ 305/446-6767 🕐 Dinner only Sat; closed Sun 🚌 42

PACIFIC TIME ($$$)

New York chef Jonathan Eismann is noted for the subtly flavored Pacific Rim cooking at this trendy Lincoln Road spot. Seafood creations draw inspiration from local ingredients and the cuisine of China and Japan.
L7 ✉ 915 Lincoln Road ☎ 305/534-5979 🚌 K, F/M, S, W

WISH ($$$)

Bizarrely enough, a once exclusively vegetarian menu now reads like a carnivore's dream of steak and chops in only-in-South-Beach forms. The memorable setting is created by designer Todd Oldham.
M7 ✉ The Hotel, 801 Collins Avenue ☎ 305/531-2222 🚌 C, H, K, W

CONTINENTAL AMERICAN

ASTOR PLACE
($$–$$$)
Stunning hotel, innovative setting. Light, bright contemporary cooking ranges from smoked, grilled cowboy prime rib to Caribbean jerk tuna.
✚ M7 ✉ 956 Washington Avenue ☎ 305/672-7217 🖵 C, H, K, W

ATLANTIC ($$$)
Way up at Surfside, this Ralph Lauren-designed restaurant in the Beach House Hotel has a view of the ocean and specializes in fish. Try the crabcakes with succotash.
✚ M6 ✉ 9449 Collins Avenue ☎ 305/695-7930 🖵 H, S

BALANS ($$)
Flavors from the Caribbean, Asia, and Mediterranean Europe pepper the menu, which also includes standbys such as grilled steak and sea bass. Tables outside.
✚ L6 ✉ 1022 Lincoln Road ☎ 305/534-9191 🖵 K, F/M, S, W

BIG PINK ($–$$)
Cheese-burgers, baby-back ribs, and creatively ethnic dishes like Mexican shrimp calzone and Thai pasta are just a few of the foods served with South Beach style and New York attitude.
✚ M8 ✉ 157 Collins Avenue ☎ 305/531-0888 🖵 H, M, W

CAFÉ MOSAIC ($$$)
Eat on the terrace of the classy National Hotel, overlooking the beautiful 1940s swimming pool. Try a mojo marinated duck crepe or Caribbean seafood stew.
✚ N6 ✉ 1677 Collins Avenue ☎ 305/423-7260 🖵 C, H, K, W

CASABLANCA ($$)
Impressive regional American and inter-national fare, including some excellent seafood.
✚ M7 ✉ 650 Ocean Drive ☎ 305/534-9463 🕐 Breakfast, lunch, dinner 🖵 C, H, K, W

CHEEKY MONKEY ($$$)
The yucca and English pea somosa appetizer gives you an idea of the imagination and flair at work in the kitchen. Here, global influences marry with a certain impishness, which is implied by the restaurant's name.
✚ M7 ✉ Blue Moon Hotel, 944 Collins Avenue ☎ 305/534-2650 🖵 C, H, K, W

RESTAURANT ST. MICHEL (SS)
This French-rooted new-American restaurant is always crowded for occasions, from Valentine's to Mother's Day. Comfortable surroundings and no cutting edge.
✚ Off map ✉ 162 Alcazar Avenue, Coral Gables ☎ 305/446-6572 🖵 42

THE FORGE ($$$)
Seventy years of history reverberate in this old-fashioned, long-time favorite. Good enough for Madonna and Michael Jordan. Over 250,000 bottles in the wine cellar.
✚ H3 ✉ 432 Arthur Godfrey Road (41st Street) ☎ 305/538-8533 🕐 Dinner only 🖵 C, G, H, L, M, S

New York, Miami-style

With more fashionable eateries than you can shake a stick at, Miami Beach also has two archetypal New York-style delicatessens that have been in business since the 1950s serving deli food at breakfast, lunch, and dinner. In South Beach, try Wolfie's (✚ M6 ✉ 2039 Collins Avenue ☎ 305/538-6626), open 24 hours, for a crowd that's part New York retirees and part late nightclubbers, enjoying great soups and real cheesecake; farther north, join the line for Wolfie Cohen's Rascal House (✚ Off map ✉ 17190 Collins Avenue ☎ 305/947-4581), the larger and louder of the two with huge portions to match.

63

MEDITERRANEAN & FRENCH

Worth noting

Many of the true stars of Miami's restaurant scene, such as Jonathan Eismann at Pacific Time (➤ 62) and Michael Schwartz at Nemo (➤ 62), are well established and likely to remain pillars of the city's gastronomic life for sometime yet. However, this is a notoriously fickle business and today's to-die-for dining rooms may flicker in and out of fashion at the drop of a wok-fried shrimp. If you have your heart set on a particular restaurant for the evening, always call ahead just to check. Reservations are strongly recommended for the most popular spots.

CAFFE ABBRACCI ($$$)

Celebrities and power diners head for this stylish top-of-the-range Italian ristorante in the Gables. Excellent veal and home-made carpaccio.
✚ Off map ✉ 318 Aragon Avenue, Coral Gables ☎ 305/441-0700 ⏰ Dinner only Sat and Sun 🚌 42

CAFFE MILANO ($$)

Strong selections of pasta and salads in unpretentious surroundings.
✚ M7 ✉ 850 Ocean Drive ☎ 305/532-0707 🚌 C, H, K, W

ESCOPAZZO ($$$)

Pino Bodoni is the host and owner of this ever-expanding South Beach favorite, where seafood and risottos are outstanding.
✚ M6 ✉ 1311 Washington Avenue ☎ 305/674-9450 ⏰ Closed Wed 🚌 C, H, K, W

LA PALME D'OR ($$$)

Savor the foods of France from a different Michelin-rated chef the first week of each month. In the Biltmore Hotel.
✚ Off map ✉ 1200 Anastasia Avenue, Coral Gables ☎ 305/445-1926 🚌 24, 42, 72

LE PROVENÇAL ($$)

The aura of France permeates in this small, family-run bistro. Many dishes make use of garlic, olive oil, and tomatoes in true Provençal style.
✚ Off map ✉ 382 Miracle Mile, Coral Gables ☎ 305/448-8984 ⏰ Closed Sun 🚌 42

LES DEUX FONTAINES ($$)

Chef Jean-Pierre Petit turns out perfectly presented French/Mediterranean cuisine, including many delicious seafood dishes.
✚ M7 ✉ Ocean Front Hotel, 1230 Ocean Drive ☎ 305/672-7878 🚌 C, H, K, W

OSTERIA DEL TEATRO ($$$)

It's elbow to elbow in Dino Pirola's tiny South Beach restaurant. North Italian cooking gets no better than this. Beef is great, pasta exceptional (look for stone crab-filled ravioli in lobster sauce), desserts a must.
✚ M6 ✉ 1443 Washington Avenue ☎ 305/538-7850 🚌 C, H, K, W

SPIGA ($$–$$$)

Romantic and discrete, this is a stylish setting for fine regional Italian dishes. Find it tucked away in the Impala Hotel.
✚ M6 ✉ 1228 Collins Avenue ☎ 305/534-0079 ⏰ Dinner only 🚌 C, H, K, W

THE STRAND ($$$)

Asian and French flavors turn up in the best South Beach eclectic style in an array of imaginative dishes. Game is popular.
✚ M8 ✉ 455 Ocean Drive ☎ 305/532-1200 🚌 H, M, W

1220 AT THE TIDES ($$$)

Arguably the best, most authentic, and most expensive French restaurant in town at the cool Tides Hotel. Dress is designer-casual. Desserts are out of this world.
✚ M6 ✉ 1220 Ocean Drive ☎ 305/604-5130 ⏰ Dinner only 🚌 H, M, W

SEAFOOD

A FISH CALLED AVALON ($$–$$$)

Lobster, king prawn, and crab legs all show up on a seafood menu here, including Florida favorites such as grilled mahi-mahi and blackened grouper.

✚ M7 ✉ Avalon Hotel, 700 Ocean Drive ☎ 305/523-1727 ◷ Dinner only ◨ C, H, K, W

BIG FISH ($$–$$$)

Top-notch seafood in a deceptively rustic setting beside the Miami River, with views of the passing cargo boats.

✚ F8 ✉ 55 S.W. Miami Avenue Road ☎ 305/373-1770 ◨ 6, 8

EAST COAST FISHERIES ($$)

Dockside on the Miami River since 1925, you won't find fresher fish. In season sample giant Florida lobster and stone crabs, as well as snapper, grouper, conch, tuna, and shrimp. Also Angus steaks and excellent Key lime pie.

✚ E8 ✉ 360 W. Flagler Street ☎ 305/372-1300 ◉ Government Center ◨ Any serving Downtown

FISH MARKET ($$$)

Seafood seldom comes better than this. Elegant setting.

✚ F6 ✉ Wyndham Hotel, 1601 Biscayne Boulevard ☎ 305/374-0000 ext 3475 ◷ Dinner only Sat; closed Sun ◉ Omni ◨ 3, 16, 32, 48, 62, C, F/M, K, S, T

FISHBONE GRILL ($–$$)

Watch the chef at work in the open kitchen and then devour a sumptuous meal—mahi-mahi, grouper, or one of the many daily specials.

✚ F8 ✉ 650 S. Miami Avenue ☎ 305/530-1915 ◷ Dinner only Sat; closed Sun ◨ 5th Street ◨ 6, 8, 24, 48, 95, B

GARCIA'S SEAFOOD GRILLE ($)

Friendly, family-run riverside eatery with daily seafood specials.

✚ E7 ✉ 398 N.W. North River Drive ☎ 305/375-0765 ◉ Government Center ◨ Any serving Downtown

JOE'S STONE CRAB ($$$)

You'll have to stand in line at this landmark to tuck into the trademark stone crabs and mustard sauce, and perfect Key lime pie.

✚ M8 ✉ 227 Biscayne Street ☎ 305/673-0365 ◷ Lunch Tue–Sat; dinner daily ◨ H, W

MONTY'S STONE CRAB RESTAURANT ($$$)

The original branch of the noted seafood eatery, now also in South Beach, is good for it's stone crabs and fish.

✚ Off map ✉ 2550 S. Bayshore Drive, Coconut Grove ☎ 305/858-1431 ◨ 48

GRILLFISH ($$)

Simplicity is the key to this lively, ultra-chic seafood specialist with a cheerful staff. Second branch in Coral Gables.

✚ M6 ✉ 1444 Collins Avenue ☎ 305/538-9908 ◨ C, H, K, W

Miami seafood

The most avidly consumed local dish is the claws of the stone crab, a large, creamy, and chewy crustacean in season from mid-October to mid-May and often very expensive. Other delights include Florida lobster and conch (pronounced "konk"), commonly served in fritters and chowders. Among popular fish are grouper, tuna, swordfish, and dolphin (as mahi-mahi is known here), often served grilled or blackened Southern style.

CUBAN & SPANISH

Cuban food

It's come a long way from Little Havana's *Calle Ocho* (8th Street, Miami), where restaurants specialize in *mojito*-laced *lecón* and *carne asada*. Trend-setters Yuca and Larios on the Beach, in fashionable Miami districts, are making waves with their innovative cuisine. But the more traditional eateries are still value for money with classic dishes of pork, chicken, or seafood, and yellow or white rice, yucca, black beans, plantains, or fried bananas on the side. Or try *loncherias* (snack bars) for Cuban toasted sandwiches: *pan con lechón*—roast pork, onions, and *mojo*; *emparedados*—ham, roast pork, cheese, and pickles on garlic-rubbed Cuban bread. Wash it all down with *café cubano*—intense sweet, black coffee in tiny cups.

CASA JUANCHO ($$)
A long-time Miami favorite, this mock-castle has heavy wood tables, tiled floors, and hearty full-flavored dishes. You could be in Spain.
✚ C9 ✉ 2436 S.W. 8th Street, Little Havana ☎ 305/642-2452 ▣ 8

CASA LARIOS ($–$$)
Take a trip to a little-touristed part of Miami to enjoy the friendly progenitor of more famous and star-studded Larios at the Beach. Traditional Cuban food is prepared and presented with flair.
✚ Off map ✉ 7705 W. Flagler Street ☎ 305/266-5494 ▣ 11

DIEGO'S RESTAURANT ($$$)
Simply-cooked Spanish dishes, such as grilled salmon and *cochinillo* (roast suckling pig). Tapas bar and outdoor dining.
✚ Off map ✉ 3555 S.W. 8th Street, Little Havana ☎ 305/444-0240 ▣ 8

EL VIAJANTE SEGUNDO ($–$$)
Cuban dishes such as palomilla steak garnished with onions and crunchy ham croquettes are served with speed to a mixed crowd of local regulars and appreciative visitors.
✚ M6 ✉ 1676 Collins Avenue ☎ 305/534-2101 ▣ C, F/M, G, H, K, L, S, W

LARIOS ON THE BEACH ($–$$)
One of several restaurants owned by Miami music stars Emilio and Gloria Estefan, this is a great place to sample new-style Cuban cuisine; in the evening, live Cuban music gets people dancing.
✚ M7 ✉ 820 Ocean Drive ☎ 305/532-9577 ▣ C, H, K, W

PUERTO SAGUA ($)
Outliving most South Beach eateries, this old-timer has a fabulous mural of Havana.
✚ M7 ✉ 700 Collins Avenue ☎ 305/673-1115 ▣ C, H, K, W

RESTAURANTE BOTIN ($$$)
A clone of the world's oldest restaurant in Madrid, with the same classic dishes: cochinillo, lamb, and paella. Long list of Spanish wines.
✚ Off map ✉ 2101 Coral Way, Little Havana ☎ 305/856-6030 ▣ 24

VERSAILLES ($)
The chandelier-lit dining room sees endless dressed-up Cuban birthday and wedding functions. It's loud, and just watching as waiters bear trayfuls of tasty and absurdly inexpensive Cuban food through the packed tables is great fun.
✚ Off map ✉ 3555 S.W. 8th Street, Little Havana ☎ 305/444-0240 ▣ 8

YUCA ($$$)
Here a cosmopolitan crowd experience what a skilled chef can do to raise Cuban basics to gastronomic heights. Rabbit comes with chocolate-based mole sauce and yucca is filled with picadillo of wild mushrooms.
✚ L7 ✉ 501 Lincoln Road ☎ 305/532-9822 ▣ K, F/M, S, W

LATIN STEAK HOUSES

CABALLO VIEJO ($$)
Venezuelan fare has yet to make an impact on Miami, which is all the more reason for sampling this lively but small eatery offering everything from plantain sandwiches to gargantuan steak dishes.
🕂 Off map ✉ 7921 S.W. 40th Street ☎ 305/256-8772 🚍 40

EL NOVILLIO ($$–$$$)
One of Miami's highly regarded Nicaraguan restaurants, El Novillio is especially popular for its flavorful *churrasco*—grilled steak.
🕂 Off map ✉ 6830 S.W. 40th Street, west of Coral Gables ☎ 305/284-8417 🚍 40

EL RANCHO GRANDE ($–$$)
An untrendy restaurant in a trendy area, offering a good range of Mexican favorites in unpretentious surroundings.
🕂 M6 ✉ 1626 Pennsylvania Avenue ☎ 305/673-0480 🚍 C, F/M, G, H, L, S

GAUCHO ROOM ($$$)
Beef and more beef, the Argentine way, cooked over oak wood. The hot sauces bring tears to your eyes. In a sophisticated hotel, with prices to match.
🕂 M6 ✉ Loews Miami Beach Hotel, 1601 Collins Avenue ☎ 305/604-5290 🕐 Dinner only; closed Mon 🚍 C, H, K, W

GUAYACAN ($$)
Nicaraguan eating at reasonable cost; the menu is strongly meat-oriented, though there are several tempting seafood choices.
🕂 C9 ✉ 1933 S.W. 8th Street ☎ 305/649-2015 🚍 8

LOS RANCHOS OF BAYSIDE ($$–$$$)
The city's most stylish and most admired Nicaraguan restaurant, with flavorful steaks and ultra-sweet desserts.
🕂 G7 ✉ Bayside Marketplace, 401 Biscayne Boulevard ☎ 305/375-0666 🚇 College/ Bayside 🚍 3, 16, 48, 95, C, S

MAMA VIEJA ($–$$)
Colombian cuisine, from seafood gumbo to beef tongue with creole sauce, in a friendly setting.
🕂 M5 ✉ 235 23rd Street ☎ 305/538-2400 🚍 C, F/M, G, H, L, S

PORCÃO ($$$)
This Brazilian restaurant centers on a buffet table groaning with beef, pork, chicken, and other meats; the salads and vegetables are almost an afterthought.
🕂 M9 ✉ Four Ambassadors, 801 S. Bayshore Drive ☎ 305/373-2777 🚍 24, 48

SEÑOR FROG'S MEXICAN GRILL ($$)
Unelaborate but lively setting for Mexican fare. Go for the sizzling fajitas.
🕂 Off map ✉ 3480 Main Highway ☎ 305/448-0999 🚇 Coconut Grove 🚍 42, 48

TANGO BEEF CAFÉ ($)
An affordable Argentine steak house, with that Buenos Aires atmosphere and first class, properly aged meats. Popular with locals.
🕂 Off map ✉ 946 Normandy Drive ☎ 305/861-7797 🕐 Call for opening hours 🚍 L

Miami menu glossary

Adobo: Cuban marinade of sour orange juice, garlic, cumin, and oregano.

Batido: Hispanic milkshake of fruit, ice, and sweetened condensed milk.

Boliche: Cuban pot roast.

Chimichurri: Sauce made from parsley, garlic, and olive oil, to go with...

Churrasco: Nicaraguan grilled marinated beef tenderloin.

Enchilado: Seafood in Cuban-style Creole sauce.

Frijoles negros: Black beans.

Lechon asado: Roast suckling pig.

Mojito: Cuban cocktail of rum, lime, yerbabuena, and soda water.

Mojo: Cuban sauce of garlic and sour orange juice.

Picadillo: Ground beef served with olives, capers, and raisins.

Tamale: Cornmeal pastry cooked in a corn husk.

Yuca: Cassava root.

ASIAN CUISINE

Alternative dining

Upscale Tantra (✉ 1445 Pennsylvania Avenue ☎ 305/672-4765) presents a startling array of Turkish, southern Mediterranean, Indian, and Middle Eastern fare complete with belly dancers and a grass-covered floor. The simpler Café Efesus (✉ 1339 Washington Avenue ☎ 305/ 674-0078) has hummus, potent coffee, and other Turkish temptations, while the German Dab Haus (✉ 852 Alton Road ☎ 305/534-9557) offers goulash soup, schnitzels, veal sausages, and more. Red Square (✉ 411 Washington Avenue ☎ 305/672-0200) serves New Russian cusine and is very good if you like caviar.

BAMBU ($$–$$$)
Actress owner Cameron Diaz is unlikely to be among the diners in this cozy spot. But the sushi and other fare from the Pan-Asian menu is sumptuous and there are plenty of takers. Very exclusive.
➕ M6 ✉ 1661 Meridian Avenue ☎ 305/531-4800
🚍 Any serving South Beach

CHINA GRILL ($$–$$$)
High-energy, new-wave Chinese pulling out all the stops. Check out lobster pancakes and crispy duck with caramelized black vinegar sauce.
➕ M8 ✉ 404 Washington Avenue ☎ 305/534-2211
🚍 H, W

CHRYSANTHEMUM ($–$$)
Delicious Szechuan and Peking cuisine. Also vegetarian options.
➕ M6 ✉ 1248 Washington Avenue ☎ 305/531-5656
🚍 C, H, K, W

HOUSE OF INDIA ($–$$)
Longstanding Gables favorite. The space is a clutter but the lunch buffet offers excellent value. Breads from the tandoori oven are delicious, and the goat and the spinach and lamb curries stand out.
➕ Off map ✉ 22 Merrick Way, Coral Gables ☎ 305/444-2348 🕐 Dinner only Sun
🚍 24, 40, 56, J

MAIKO ($$)
A good bet for Japanese cuisine promising a good range of sushi; try sushi-sashimi combination.
➕ M6 ✉ 1255 Washington Avenue ☎ 305/531-6369
🚍 C, H, K, W

OPIUM ($$$)
With its hip East-meets-West decor, this is a showcase for Pan-Asian cooking at its best, from red Thai chicken curry with roasted pineapple to Szechuan peppercorn-crusted steak. The determinedly cool clientele are predominately of South Beach somebodies.
➕ M8 ✉ 136 Collins Avenue ☎ 305/674-8630 🕐 Dinner only; closed Mon, Tue 🚍 H, M, W

THAI TONI ($$)
The many Thai favorites have a South Beach accent at this cozy place with a clientele of trendy clubbers, food mavens, and choosy tourists.
➕ M7 ✉ 890 Washington Avenue ☎ 305/538-8424
🕐 Dinner only 🚍 C, H, K, W

TONI'S SUSHI BAR ($$)
Long-established and deservedly popular for the freshest of fish and eye-catching presentation. Fine noodle and vegetarian dishes. Open late.
➕ M6 ✉ 1208 Washington Avenue ☎ 305/673-9368
🕐 Dinner only 🚍 C, H, K, W

WOK & ROLL ($)
This fashionable South Beach Chinese restaurant stands out in the crowd. You can watch your food being prepared in the open kitchen. The soups are good, but so is the array of dim sum and the flavorsome garlic pork.
➕ M6 ✉ 1451 Collins Avenue ☎ 305/672-0911 🚍 C, H, K, W

PEOPLE-WATCHING CAFÉS

CAFÉ TU-TU TANGO ($–$$)
It's fun to graze at this arty Grove tapas bar. The sangria's great and the crowd cosmopolitan, and it's easy to order too many of the eclectic offerings.
✚ Off map ✉ CocoWalk, 3015 Grand Avenue, Coconut Grove ☎ 305/529-2222 🚇 Coconut Grove 🚌 42, 48

CASA SALSA ($$$)
Owned by Latin heartthrob Ricky Martin, this place has a menu of Puerto Rican fare, but the accent is on fun as much as food, with live salsa and enough rum to sink a navy.
✚ M7 ✉ 524 Ocean Drive ☎ 305/604-5959 🚌 C, H, K, W

FRONT PORCH CAFÉ ($)
Salads, sandwiches, pizzas, and daily specials prepared with style and served without fuss inside or out.
✚ M6 ✉ 1424 Ocean Drive ☎ 305/531-8300 🕐 Breakfast, lunch, dinner 🚌 C, H, K, W

GREEN STREET CAFÉ ($)
One of the first sidewalk cafés in Bohemian Coconut Grove. First-class coffee, light meals. A local haunt.
✚ Off map ✉ 3110 Commodore Plaza, Coconut Grove ☎ 305/567-0662 🚌 C, H, K, W

JOFFREY'S COFFEE CO. ($)
On the corner of Euclid Avenue and Lincoln Road, Joffrey's has plenty of outdoor tables where you can sip various flavors of coffee and munch pastries.
✚ M6 ✉ 660 Lincoln Road ☎ 305/673-5474 🕐 Breakfast, lunch, dinner 🚌 K, F/M, S, W

NEWS CAFÉ ($)
In the plush Mayfair Shops, the Coconut Grove branch is where locals come for breakfast and their international newspapers. The sister café at South Beach has nimbly crafted salads and sandwiches, and is ideally placed to watch the beach-side procession.
✚ Off map; M7 ✉ 2901 Florida Avenue, Coconut Grove; 800 Ocean Drive ☎ 305/774-6397; 305/538-6397 🚌 48; C, H, K, W

PELICAN CAFÉ ($$)
Cameron Diaz, Antonio Banderas, Johnny Depp; they've all eaten in this indoor and outdoor café at the funkiest hotel in town. Try the Pelican chocolate cake.
✚ M7 ✉ 826 Ocean Drive ☎ 305/673-3373 🚌 C, H, K, W

TERRACE AT THE TIDES ($$)
Sit under the sunshades, pretend you're a star, and look down on the passing parade along Ocean Drive. Excellent French pastries. No reservations.
✚ M7 ✉ The Tides Hotel, 1220 Ocean Drive ☎ 305/604-5070 🚌 C, H, K, W

VAN DYKE CAFÉ ($)
Enormously popular for people-watching, with burgers, eggs Benedict, and sandwiches.
✚ L7 ✉ 846 Lincoln Road ☎ 305/534-3600 🕐 Breakfast, lunch, dinner 🚌 K, F/M, S, W

Family fun
Miami is full of restaurants that are family-friendly, and a lot of fun as well. Youngsters always enjoy themed restaurants such as Hard Rock Café (✉ Bayside Market, Biscayne Boulevard ☎ 305/377-3110) and Johnny Rockets (✉ 3036 Grand Avenue, Coconut Grove; 728 Ocean Drive, South Beach ☎ 305/444-1000; 305/538-2115). Star-struck kids want to go to Bongos Cuban Café (✉ 601 Biscayne Boulevard ☎ 786/777-2100), Gloria Estefan's latest eatery at the American Airlines Arena downtown, and Casa Salsa (➤ 69), where everyone hopes to spot owner Ricky Martin. For on the spot entertainment, try Baraboo (✉ 7300 Ocean Terrace ☎ 305/867-4242), where waiters perform magic tricks. But, for sheer nostalgia, you can't beat the landmark 11th Street Diner (1065 Washington Avenue ☎ 305/534-6373), with its excellent burgers and ice creams.

Department Stores & Malls

Miami International Arts & Design District

Around the junction of N. Miami Avenue and N.E. 40th Street, north of Downtown, are the dozens of contemporary design stores forming the Miami International Arts & Design District. Most offer expensive, beautiful furnishings and decorative items for the home; a few also offer clothing. On the second Friday of each month, an evening Gallery Walk finds store owners and designers on hand to talk about their wares.

AVENTURA MALL
Big and pleasantly arranged indoor shopping mall with major stores such as Macy's, Sears, and JCPenney among more than 200 retail outlets.
⊞ Off map ✉ 19501 Biscayne Boulevard, North Miami ☎ 305/935-1110 ▣ 3, 9, E, S

BAL HARBOUR SHOPS
Nestled amid the lush tropical vegetation of this landscaped mall are big-spenders' favorites such as Gucci, Cartier, and Vuitton, alongside Saks Fifth Avenue, and Neiman Marcus.
⊞ Off map ✉ 9700 Collins Avenue, Miami Beach ☎ 305/866-0311 ▣ G, K, R, S

BAYSIDE MARKETPLACE
Adjacent to Downtown with free entertainment, Bayside Marketplace is a well-designed and enjoyable mall, with wonderful views across Biscayne Bay.
⊞ G7 ✉ 401 Biscayne Boulevard ☎ 305/577-3344 ▣ College/Bayside ▣ 3, 16, 48, 95, C, S

BURDINES
This is the original home of Miami's oldest department store. It was established in 1898 and is still stocking just about everything you might need, from clothing to kitchenware, here and in its many branches.
⊞ F8 ✉ 22 E. Flagler Street ☎ 305/577-2312 ▣ Miami Avenue ▣ Any serving Downtown

COCOWALK
This funny and fashionable conglomeration of restaurants and stores, with a movie complex, is at its liveliest and most enjoyable on the busy weekends.
⊞ Off map ✉ 3015 Grand Avenue, Coconut Grove ☎ 305/444-0777 ▣ Coconut Grove ▣ 42, 48

DADELAND MALL
A mall of mind-boggling size, this is home to immense branches of Burdines, Saks Fifth Avenue, and JCPenney, plus specialty stores and restaurants.
⊞ Off map ✉ 7535 N. Kendall Drive, Kendall ☎ 305/665-6226 ▣ Dadeland South ▣ 1, 52, 73, 87, 88

DOLPHIN MALL
This Miami newcomer dwarfs its rivals with more than 200 mostly discount stores, an indoor amusement park, a huge multi-screen movie complex, and an innovative setting west of the airport.
⊞ Off map ✉ Nr junction of N.W. 107th Street and State Road 836 ☎ 707/224-3795

THE FALLS SHOPPING CENTER
This pleasant outdoor mall, which meanders around streams, fountains, lakes, and waterfalls, is home to Bloomingdales, Walking Company, and lots more.
⊞ Off map ✉ 8888 Howard Drive, Kendall area ☎ 305/255-4570 ▣ 52, 57

LOEHMANNS'S FASHION ISLAND

Loehmann's, a noted discount outlet for fashionable women's clothing, gives its name to this workmanlike conglomeration of stores and restaurants. Other places to spend money include a massive branch of Barnes & Noble booksellers and a Publix supermarket dependably stocked with all affordable essentials. A visit to the 16-screen movie theater provides an alternative diversion.

✚ Off map ✉ Biscayne Boulevard at 187th Street, North Miami ☎ 305/932-0520 🚍 3, 9, E, S

THE MALL AT 163RD STREET

A pretty average collection of shops and department stores selling fashion, sportswear, toys, and music—but where else can you walk on the world's first Teflon-coated floor?

✚ Off map ✉ 1421 N.E. 163rd Street, North Miami ☎ 305/947-9845 🚍 2, 16, 75, 83, 95, V

MIAMI INTERNATIONAL MALL

Burdines and JCPenney are among the department stores here, along with some 150 specialty stores, a food court, and a movie complex. The mall's privilege card can bring discounts for high-spending tourists.

✚ Off map ✉ 1455 N.W. 107th Avenue ☎ 305/593-1775 🚍 7, 71

OMNI INTERNATIONAL MALL

The decent selection of electronic goods stores are particularly popular with visitors from Latin America. There's also Downtown's only movie theater and an old-fashioned carousel.

✚ F6 ✉ 1601 Biscayne Boulevard ☎ 305/374-6664 🚇 Omni 🚍 3, 16, 32, 48, 62, C, F/M, K, S, T

SHOPS AT SUNSET PALACE

Open-air, three-level shopping area with big name stores such as NikeTown and Virgin Megastore, smaller ones like toy purveyor FAO Schwarz and the wacky furniture-seller Z Gallerie, plus a 24-screen movie theater, GameWorks, and IMAX theater. The location hosts a nightly laser show and other free live entertainment.

✚ Off map ✉ Intersection of US-1 and Red Road (57th Avenue) ☎ 305/663-0873 🚇 South Miami 🚍 57, 65, 72

STREETS OF MAYFAIR

Patterned tiles, fountains, and assorted statuary create a Mediterranean mood at this mazelike three-building collection of chic boutiques, art galleries, and other diversions for the well-heeled. Come evening, attention switches to the tight cluster of eateries, nightclubs, and entertainment venues.

✚ Off map ✉ 2911 Grand Avenue, Coconut Grove ☎ 305/448-1700 🚇 Coconut Grove 🚍 42, 48

Shopping districts

Miami has several well defined shopping areas. Along Coral Gables' Miracle Mile, upscale antiques, books, and specialties can be found alongside numerous bridal shops. Coconut Grove's CocoWalk is only the focal point of a pack of retail outlets offering everything from jeans to designer jewelry. Miami Beach's Lincoln Road mixes fashion boutiques, books, gifts, and groovy lighting and homeware stores with art galleries, plus a great selection of outdoor cafés and restaurants. Many established and aspirant clothing designers have outlets in South Beach, mostly on Washington and Collins avenues between 7th and 12th streets.

CLOTHES & ACCESSORIES

Essential skates

Passing yourself off as a local in South Beach is hard to do without a pair of in-line skates attached to your feet and the skills necessary to stay upright and moving. A wide range of skates can be found at Fritz's Skate Shop (✉ 726 Lincoln Road ☎ 305/532 1954) and Skate 2000 (✉ 1200 Ocean Drive ☎ 305/538 8282).

ARMANI EXCHANGE
Local branch of the internationally renowned designer of quality, stylish men's and womenswear. Look for the glass block facade, neon-lit at night.
➕ M7　✉ 760 Collins Avenue　☎ 305/531-5900　🚇 C, H, K, W

BEATNIX
Stand out from the crowd by donning a bright orange jumper, a dayglo T-shirt or any combination of the distincive multicolor clothing creations that are sold here.
➕ M7　✉ 1149 Washington Avenue　☎ 305/532-8733　🚇 C, H, K, W

CHOCOLATE BIKINIS
If you want to be noticed on the beach, sort through the collection of daringly designed and boldly colored bikinis, and other beachwear filling these racks. Chocoholics may be disappointed.
➕ Off map　✉ 3082 Grand Avenue, Coconut Grove　☎ 305/441-9103　🚇 Coconut Grove　🚌 42, 48

CINDERELLA BOUTIQUE
Toddlers and near-teens emerge well-dressed from this top-class children's clothing outlet—and their parents will be poorer.
➕ Off map　✉ 329 Miracle Mile, Coral Gables　☎ 305/442-0379　🚌 24, 40, 56, J

CORAL GABLES BRIDALS
Check out the sumptuous wedding outfits in stores along Coral Gables' Miracle Mile. This is just one among several bridal specialists filled with dazzling dresses, bridesmaid's outfits, and other must-have creations and concoctions for the big day, including multitiered wedding cakes.
➕ Off map　✉ 366 Miracle Mile, Coral Gables　☎ 305/445-5896　🚌 24, 40, 56, J

FLY BOUTIQUE
Well worth a browse for new and used designer clothing, from business suits to club wear, at tempting prices; also a stash of wacky jewelry.
➕ M6　✉ 650 Lincoln Road　☎ 305/604-8508　🚇 K, F/M, S, W

FRONT PAGE
Pricey but generally fine men's and women's garments to suit the daring dresser. This is a good first stop en route to a fashion-conscious South Beach nightspot.
➕ M7　✉ 1127 Washington Avenue　☎ 305/532-5494　🚇 C, H, K, W

INTERMIX
This New York boutique has brought its youthful sass to SoBe. In addition to its own lines, the store stocks clothes by today's hottest designers, from John Bartlett and Jimmy Choo to Malia Mills and Chloe.
➕ M7　✉ 634 Collins Avenue　☎ 305/531-5950　🚇 C, H, K, W

J.W. COOPER'S
A pseudo log cabin with an extensive stock of jeans, belts, boots, and

buckles, to create that oh-so-fashionable cowboy look.

✚ Off map ✉ CocoWalk, 3015 Grand Avenue, Coconut Grove ☎ 305/441-1380 🚇 Coconut Grove 🚌 42, 48

LA CASA DE DUAYABERAS

Comfortable and ideally suited to warm climes, the billowing Cuban shirts known as guayaberas, so loved by elderly Cuban men strolling Little Havana, also make a sensible purchase for visitors to wear around town and take home as a souvenir. Buy off the peg or made to measure.

✚ Off map ✉ 5840 S.W. 8th Street ☎ 305/266-9683 🚌 8

MIAMI TWICE

Beguilingly vast selection of lovely vintage clothing and accessories for men and women, including daring items such as high-rise platform shoes and over-sized rings. Also furniture, antiques, and Americana.

✚ M6 ✉ 6562 S.W. 40th Street ☎ 305/666-0127 🚌 K, F/M, S, W

OM JEWELRY

Hundreds of imaginative items.

✚ Off map ✉ 3070 Grand Avenue, Coconut Grove ☎ 305/445-1865 🚇 Coconut Grove 🚌 42, 48

RIVOLI EXECUTIVE HANDBAGS

A haven for the woman who simply must have the right handbag at any price.

✚ Off map ✉ 299 Miracle Mile, Coral Gables ☎ 305/443-7373 🚇 Coconut Grove 🚌 24, 40, 56, J

SEYBOLD BUILDING

Originally a bakery, this 10-story 1920s building now houses scores of jewelry vendors; look for watches, gold, and diamond rings with settings from classic to contemporary.

✚ F7 ✉ 39 E. Flagler Street ☎ 305/377-0122 🚇 Miami Avenue 🚌 Any serving Downtown

SNOWS

Refusing anything as vulgar as advertising, this top-of-the-range jewelry store has built a deservedly excellent reputation through word of mouth since 1959.

✚ Off map ✉ 299 Miracle Mile, Coral Gables ☎ 305/443-7373 🚌 24, 40, 56, J

THEE LEATHERY

Venerable purveyor of fine backpacks, hiking shoes, and leather jackets worn by some Miami clubbers just for show.

✚ Off map ✉ 3460 Main Highway, Coconut Grove ☎ 305/448-5711 🚇 Coconut Grove 🚌 42, 48

VERSACE JEANS COUTURE

South Beach branch of the international jet set's favorite dress-down designer clothing outlet; stylish togs at high prices and some locally inspired accessories such as Florida motif earrings.

✚ M7 ✉ 755 Washington Avenue ☎ 305/532-5993 🚌 C, H, K, W

Souvenir hunting

Miami is a glorious repository of all that is best—or possibly worst depending on your taste—about Florida souvenir hunting. South Beach is the unassailable capital of tongue-in-cheek stores positively awash with Floridiana in all its palm tree, flamingo, and alligator motif splendor. The Bayside Marketplace and Coconut Grove run a close second and third. For something less tacky, check out Lincoln Road's Antiques and Collectibles Market on the second and fourth Sundays of the month. You never know what might turn up.

ANTIQUES & COLLECTIBLES

COLLECTION PRIVÉE DE PEINTURE ET DE SCULPTURE
With a few thousand dollars to spare you might be able to pick up a modest knick-knack from this determinedly upscale purveyor of paintings and sculpture; major pieces cost much more.
✚ L6 ✉ 918 Lincoln Road ☎ 305/778-1888 🖥 K, F/M, S, W

THE CURIO SHOP ANTIQUES GALLERY
European and American antiques and objets d'art, most from the 18th and 19th centuries.
✚ Off map ✉ 349 Miracle Mile, Coral Gables ☎ 305/444-7234 🖥 24, 40, 56, J

LUNATIKA
Inventively designed lamps such as the Sputnik chandelier, paper lanterns, and other cutting edge items for the home.
✚ L6 ✉ 900 Lincoln Road ☎ 305/534-8585 🖥 K, F/M, S, W

MACASSAR
Art, ornaments, furniture, and many more fine original and reproduction items from India, China, Indonesia, and Thailand.
✚ M6 ✉ 445 Española Way ☎ 305/695-8086 🖥 C, H, K, W

MAYAHATCHA
This floor-to-ceiling collection from Central and South America, Africa, and Asia includes masks, incense, oils, hammocks, cookware, and lots more.
✚ Off map ✉ 3058 Grand Avenue, Coconut Grove ☎ 305/443-9040 🖥 42, 48

The Gallery Walk
If you're a comparative novice art collector and want to to get the measure of Lincoln Road's many art galleries, join the Gallery Walk, held on the second Saturday evening of each month, which covers 28 local galleries. For details of the walk, and many other Lincoln Road events, consult the *Miami Herald*.

MEXICRAFT
Steer skulls and Native American artifacts feature here among the furnishings and decorative items from colonial-era Mexico and the American Southwest.
✚ Off map ✉ 8880 S.W. 129th Terrace ☎ 305/378-0377

MOON DANCE
Here you'll find Egyptian hookahs, 19th-century Burmese Buddha images, and other old, strange, and usually very expensive collectibles.
✚ L7 ✉ 815 Lincoln Road ☎ 305/534-7772 🖥 K, F/M, S, W

POP
A delightful collection of mass-culture knick-knacks from vintage refrigerator magnets to 1960s TV show annuals.
✚ M7 ✉ 1151 Washington Avenue ☎ 305/604-9604 🖥 C, H, K, W

SENZATEMPO
Stupendous assortment of distinctively designed furniture and household items from decades past, plus fine vintage clocks and watches.
✚ M6 ✉ 1655 Meridian Avenue ☎ 305/534-5588 🖥 24, 40, 56, J

SOUTH FLORIDA ART CENTER
This collection of studios and galleries is just the place to spot emerging artists.
✚ L6 ✉ 924 Lincoln Road ☎ 305/674-8278 🖥 K, F/M, S, W

BOOKS

B. DALTON BOOKSELLER

Comprehensively stocked general bookstore that is ideal for mainstream titles often at discount prices, and carrying a strong range of business-management and computer-related stock.

✚ Off map ✉ CocoWalk, 3015 Grand Avenue, Coconut Grove ☎ 305/444-5143 🚇 Coconut Grove 🚌 42, 48

BARNES & NOBLE

The many miles of shelving here are packed with fiction and nonfiction titles plus a formidable assortment of local, regional, and a few international newspapers; an inviting café adjoins.

✚ Off map ✉ 152 Miracle Mile, Coral Gables ☎ 305/446-4152 🚌 24, 40, 56, J

BOOKS & BOOKS

Compact but very comprehensively stocked with general titles, an excellent selection of books about Miami, and books by Miami-based authors. Friendly staff will help you find what you need.

✚ Off map ✉ 265 Aragon Avenue, Coral Gables ☎ 305/442-4408 🚌 24, 40, 56, J

BORDERS BOOKS & MUSIC

One of several city branches of the nationwide chain offers books and magazines on all subjects.

✚ Off map ✉ 3390 Mary Street, Coconut Grove ☎ 305/447-1655 🚇 Coconut Grove 🚌 42, 48

EUTOPIA

Anyone popping in to grab a book for the beach could well end up spending hours poring through the copiously filled shelves laden with books of all kinds. The store is especially strong on fiction and Florida titles.

✚ L6 ✉ 1626 Jefferson Avenue ☎ 305/532-8680 🚌 C, H, K, W

KAFKA'S KAFE

This groovy South Beach cyber café offers tens of thousands of used books and a broad stock of beyond-Florida newspapers alongside its internet terminals.

✚ M6 ✉ 1464 Washington Avenue ☎ 305/673-9669 🚌 C, H, K, W

MURDER ON MIAMI BEACH

New and used crime, mysteries, and assorted whodunnits dominate this bookstore, which also has a few collectible editions signed by their authors. Some visiting writers have left their signatures, and some their handprints, on a back wall.

✚ Off map ✉ 16850 Collins Avenue ☎ 305/956-7770 🚌 E, K, S, V

NEWS CAFÉ

A popular South Beach hangout that offers a modest selection of fiction with a stronger stock of U.S. and international newspapers.

✚ M7 ✉ 800 Ocean Drive ☎ 305/538-6397 🚌 C, H, K, W

Author readings and signings

Many Miami bookstores regularly have nationally known authors reading, discussing, and signing copies of their latest work. The guests and their subjects are as varied as the titles on the shelves, covering everything from UFO experiences to advanced management techniques. The individual stores, the freebie *Miami New Times* and the Friday *Miami Herald*, can provide the latest details.

Storytime

Younger children not smitten by Miami's charms might relish a few hours in one of the city's general bookstores that offer free storytelling sessions, sometimes with costumed characters narrating. Local newspapers have details about forthcoming events; those regularly staging such activities include the various branches of Borders Books & Music and Barnes & Noble.

BARGAINS

Publix supermarkets

In the South Beach branch of this Florida-based supermarket, known for its low prices, check out the neon-lit early 1960s architecture and look for glamorous faces jostling for position in the checkout lines.

✉ 1045 Dade Boulevard
☎ 305/534-4621

DETAILS

If nothing seems affordable elsewhere in the Miami Design District, drop into this clearance center, which on Saturdays offers reduced prices on designer furniture, lighting, and accessories.

✚ F4 ✉ 3227 N.E. 2nd Avenue ☎ 305/571-9055
🚌 9, 10

FLORIDA KEYS FACTORY SHOPS

A landscaped collection of discount stores on Miami's southern extremity with outlets for cut-price clothing, hardware, and books.

✚ Off map ✉ 250 E. Palm Drive, Homestead ☎ 305/248-4727 🚌 70

GALERIA INTERNACIONAL MALL

This effervescent Downtown mall draws mainly Latin American tourists, mostly seeking clothing and electrical goods unavailable at home—or much cheaper.

✚ F8 ✉ 255 Flagler Street
☎ 305/371-4536 🚇 Miami Avenue 🚌 Any serving Downtown

GOLDEN GLADES INDOOR FLEA MARKET

Air-conditioning makes browsing a comfort in this market comprising 150 stalls selling every type of merchandise you can think of under one roof.

✚ Off map ✉ 1313 N.W. 167th Street ☎ 305/826-3532
🚇 Golden Glades 🚌 22, 42, 77, E

MALL OF THE AMERICAS

Some of the most dependable names in retailing, such as TJ Maxx and Home Depot, are represented in this sizeable mall where virtually every shop offers goods at lower-than-normal rates.

✚ Off map ✉ 7795 W. Flagler Street ☎ 305/261-8772
🚌 87

MARUCHI CLOTHING OUTLET

Stylish threads from top designers, mostly for women, often at half or more off their normal retail price.

✚ Off map ✉ 7861 S.W. 40th Street ☎ 305/266-7136
🚌 40

OPA-LOCKA/HIALEAH FLEA MARKET

An immense flea market with over 1,000 stalls, many offering wholesale prices.

✚ Off map ✉ 12705 N.W. 42nd Avenue ☎ 305/688-8080 🚌 28, 42

SAWGRASS MILLS

Miamians do not flinch at motoring the hour-long drive to the country's largest collection of factory outlet stores. Once arrived they are liable to spend a full day browsing and buying among the scores of well-known names and specialty stores.

✚ Off map ✉ 12801 W. Sunrise Boulevard
☎ 800/FLMILLS

MISCELLANEOUS

ESPERANTO MUSIC
Rare is the musical genre not present in this colossal stock of CDs, records, and music-related publications catering to cult and mainstream interests from Cuban salsa to London techno.
✚ M6 ✉ 513 Lincoln Road ☎ 305/534-2003 🖰 K, F/M, S

THE FRAGRANCE SHOP
If you've never been able to find the right perfume, come here and make your own using the store's bottles of undiluted oils.
✚ M6 ✉ 612 Lincoln Avenue ☎ 305/535-0037 🖰 K, F/M, S, W

PERFUMANIA
One of several Miami branches of a perfume retailer well stocked with major brands at some substantial discounts.
✚ G7 ✉ 401 Biscayne Boulevard ☎ 305/577-0032 🚇 College/Bayside 🖰 3, 16, 48, 95, C, S

PINK PALM
Many unusual gifts, greetings cards, posters, and much more, filling every nook and cranny.
✚ M6 ✉ 737 Lincoln Road ☎ 305/538-8373 🖰 K, F/M, S, W

SOUTH BEACH STYLE
Everything for the style-conscious South Beach home, from art-deco sofas and dining tables to attractive stationery sets, candles, and gift items.
✚ M6 ✉ 1020 Lincoln Road ☎ 305/538-8277 🖰 K, F/M, S, W

SPY WORLD
Concealed bugging devices, miniature cameras, night-vision binoculars, and bulletproof vests.
✚ Off map ✉ 129 Miracle Mile, Coral Gables ☎ 305/442-9999 🖰 24, 40, 56, J

THINGS REMEMBERED
Personalized gift store where they will engrave your keepsakes. Other branches at N.W. 107 Avenue and Dixie Highway.
✚ Off map ✉ 19575 Biscayne Boulevard, Aventura Mall ☎ 305/932-7478 🖰 3, 9, E, S

WICK
Scented candles, fancy candleholders and candelabras, plus bath oils and other items for the home.
✚ M6 ✉ 1661 Michigan Avenue ☎ 305/538-7022 🖰 K, F/M, S, W

X-ISLE SURF SHOP
Surfboards, wetsuits, and everything else for the beach and breakers with products by many leading names.
✚ M8 ✉ 437 Washington Avenue ☎ 305/673-5900 🖰 C, H, K, W

9TH CHAKRA
Spirit-enhancing jewelry, incense, tarot cards, crystals, oils, and esoteric books. An in-house psychic is on hand to consult on your metaphysical journey.
✚ M6 ✉ 817 Lincoln Road ☎ 305/538-0671 🖰 K, F/M, S, W

Smoker's choice

Cuba's tobacco industry and the many Cubans resident in Miami conspire to make the city one of the best places in the United States to find fine cigars. Although importing genuine Cuban cigars is illegal, discerning smokers find much to please at the Macabi Cigar Shop (✉ 3473 S.W. 8th Street ☎ 305/446-2606); Stogie's (✉ 11612 S.W. 88th Street ☎ 305/598-9820); Cigar Connection (✉ 534 Lincoln Road Mall); and Zelicks Tobacco (✉ 326 Lincoln Road ☎ 305/538-1544).

CLASSICAL MUSIC & PERFORMING ARTS

Tickets

Ticketmaster (☎ 305/358-5885) can supply tickets for most major events in and around Miami. Tickets must be paid for by credit card over the telephone.

AMERICAN AIRLINES ARENA

Opened to considerable acclaim at the dawn of the new millennium, this multi-purpose waterfront auditorium seating 20,000 stages major concerts and other large-scale arts events.

✚ F/G6 ✉ 601 Biscayne Boulevard ☎ 786/777-1000 🚇 Omni International Mall 🚌 Any serving Omni International Mall

COLONY THEATER

An art-deco landmark originally built by Paramount Studios as a movie theater in 1934. Restored and reopened in 1976, the Colony now makes an intimate setting for chamber music and dance shows; many deco fittings remain intact.

✚ L6 ✉ 1040 Lincoln Road ☎ 305/674-1040 🚌 C, H, G, L, F/M, S, W

DADE COUNTY AUDITORIUM

With seating for 2,500, this is an inviting mid-sized showcase for the Miami City Ballet and the Florida Grand Opera, as well as many other performing arts events year-round.

✚ A8 ✉ 2901 W. Flagler Street, west of Downtown ☎ 305/547-5414 🚌 11

EDGE THEATER

Edgy drama, comedy, and uncategorizeable performance pieces find a home in this tiny space, seating only 49.

✚ M6 ✉ 405 Española Way ☎ 305/531-6803 🚌 C, H, K, W

GUSMAN CENTER FOR THE PERFORMING ARTS

Programing is diverse in this sumptuous, beautifully restored 1920s theater, including concerts by the New World Symphony Orchestra and many of the country's best mid-sized performing arts troupes.

✚ F8 ✉ 174 E. Flagler Street ☎ 305/374-2444 🚇 Miami Avenue 🚌 Any serving Downtown

GUSMAN CONCERT HALL

This 600-seat venue has excellent acoustics; it hosts the Miami Chamber Symphony Orchestra and other chamber recitals.

✚ Off map ✉ 1314 Miller Drive, Coral Gables ☎ 305/284-2438 🚇 University 🚌 48, 52, 72

JACKIE GLEASON THEATER FOR THE PERFORMING ARTS

Touring orchestras and opera companies appear, and the American Ballet Theater opens its touring season here in January.

✚ M5 ✉ 1700 Washington Avenue ☎ 305/673-7300 🚌 C, H, G, L, F/M, S, W

LINCOLN THEATER

The home of the New World Symphony Orchestra, the United States' premier training orchestra for talented young musicians who perform from October to May.

✚ M6 ✉ 555 Lincoln Road ☎ 305/673-3330 🚌 C, H, G, L, F/M, S, W

THEATER

ACTORS' PLAYHOUSE

From Broadway spectaculars to more introspective offerings, this splendidly restored art-deco theater mounts varied fare in its 600-seat main hall.

Off map ✉ 280 Miracle Mile, Coral Gables ☎ 305/444-9293 🚍 24, 40, 56, J

COCONUT GROVE PLAYHOUSE

Diverse dramatic works, from classical to contemporary, are staged year-round in this attractive 1920s Mediterranean-style theater, originally built to show movies. Showing live drama since the 1960s, the Playhouse earned national kudos by staging the first U.S. production of Beckett's *Waiting For Godot*; the small Encore Room hosts experimental work.

Off map ✉ 3500 Main Highway, Coconut Grove ☎ 305/442-4000 🚇 Coconut Grove 🚍 42, 48

GABLESTAGE

This gem of a theater inside the historic Biltmore Hotel (▶ 26) is the latest home of the highly regarded Florida Shakespeare Theater, which mounts several major productions each year in this intimate 154-seat auditorium. Also look out for contemporary productions and Florida premieres of Tony Award-winning productions.

Off map ✉ Biltmore Hotel, 1200 Anastasia Avenue, Coral Gables ☎ 305/445-1119 🚍 24, 42, 72

JERRY HERMAN RING THEATER

The University of Miami's major dramatic space. The program includes student and professional shows, and deserving works by lesser-known playwrights.

Off map ✉ 1380 Miller Drive, Coral Gables ☎ 305/284-3355 🚇 University 🚍 48, 52, 72

THE LITTLE STAGE

A cozy niche where you can sample the creations of aspiring playwrights, mostly performed by small, local casts and mixing humor with more avant-garde works.

M5 ✉ Acorns Civic Theater, 2100 Washington Avenue ☎ 305/673-7730 or 305/673-7817 🚍 G, K

NEW THEATER

A comfortable venue with a mixed repertoire of classical and contemporary productions, plus a few comedies.

Off map ✉ 65 Almeria Avenue, Coral Gables ☎ 305/443-5909 🚍 42, 56, J

THEATRO AVANTE

For something a little different, the Avante showcases classic and comtemporary Spanish language plays with English subtitles, and hosts an informal International Hispanic Theater Festival.

Off map ✉ 235 Alcazar Avenue, Coral Gables ☎ 305/443-8877 🚍 42, 56, J

Spanish-language theater

Miami's thriving Spanish-language theater scene often explores aspects of Cuba and the Cuban exile experience, and mounts more mainstream fare. For details look in English-language newspapers as well as the Friday *El Nuevo Herald*. Established venues include Bellas Artes (✉ 2173 S.W. 8th Street ☎ 305/325-0515); Teatro Avanti (✉ 235 Alcazar Avenue ☎ 305/445-8877); and the multi-stage Marti (✉ 420 S.W. 8th Street ☎ 305/545-7866).

LIVE MUSIC VENUES

Latin music venues

With its enormous Latin American population, Miami has numerous venues for samba, salsa, merengue, and many other musical forms from South and Central America and the Caribbean. Check out Casa Salsa (► 69); La Cavacha (✉ 10730 N.W. 25th Street ☎ 305/594-3717); Mojito Room (✉ 136 Collins Avenue ☎ 305/531-7181); and Studio 23 (✉ 247 23rd Street ☎ 305/538-1196)

BAYSIDE MARKETPLACE
One of the best places to find free samba, salsa, reggae, or rock is during the afternoon at this landscaped open-air shopping mall (► 70).
✚ G7 ✉ 401 Biscayne Boulevard ☎ 305/577-3344 🚇 College/Bayside 🚌 3, 16, 48, 95, C, S

CAFÉ NOSTALGIA AT THE FORGE
The nostalgia is for the nightlife of pre-revolutionary Cuba, re-created here with a band few can resist dancing to after imbibing a powerful mojito or two.
✚ N3 ✉ 432 41st Street ☎ 305/604-9895 🚌 G, H, L, S, T

CHURCHILL'S HIDEAWAY
Poky and smoky, this is a popular long-running venue for the best local indie rock, heavy metal, R&B, and more; many local bands cut their teeth here before graduating to bigger things.
✚ F2 ✉ 5501 N.E. 2nd Avenue, north of Downtown ☎ 305/757-1807 🚌 9, 10

CLEVELANDER
Rock and infectious Latin dance rhythm spill across Ocean Drive from the outside bar at this art-deco hotel facing the beach.
✚ M7 ✉ 1020 Ocean Drive ☎ 305/531-3485 🚌 C, H, K, W

DICK'S LAST RESORT
The local branch of this growing nationwide chain of inexpensive eateries has live rock music on Fridays and Saturdays.
✚ G7 ✉ Bayside Marketplace, 401 Biscayne Boulevard ☎ 305/375-6575 🚇 Bayside 🚌 23, 16, 48, 95, C, S

DOC DAMMER'S
Accomplished jazz combos usually appear in this restaurant venue four nights a week.
✚ Off map ✉ Hyatt Hotel, 180 Aragon Avenue, Coral Gables ☎ 305/569-6511 🚌 24, 40, 56, J

HUNGRY SAILOR
Bizarre but appealing English pub (with warm beer and draught Guiness) with a live reggae sound track. Also rock and open-mike nights. Lively crowd.
✚ Off map ✉ 3426 Main Highway, Coconut Grove ☎ 305/444-9359 🚇 Coconut Grove 🚌 42, 48

JAZID
Candlelit, appealingly intimate club with live jazz and blues. Chill out to sounds that ring the changes from trad to swing.
✚ M6 ✉ 1332 Washington Avenue ☎ 305/673-9372 🚌 C, H, K, W

MARTINI BAR
This upscale hip lounge is a good place to listen to jazz, blues, and swing music while sipping a martini.
✚ Off map ✉ 3390 Mary Street ☎ 305/444-5911 🚇 Coconut Grove 🚌 42, 48

MONTY'S RAW BAR
Infectiously rhythmic live bands from the

Caribbean and South America appear nightly in this adjunct to Monty's Stone Crab Restaurant (➤ 65). ✚ Off map ✉ 2550 S. Bayshore Drive, Coconut Grove ☎ 305/858-1431 🚇 Coconut Grove 🚌 42, 48

OLD CUTLER OYSTER CO.

Lively joint offering live music Wed–Sun. Check ahead for what's on and take your pick from country and western nights with a side order of line dancing to good old rock and roll. ✚ Off map ✉ 18415 S. Dixie Highway ☎ 305/238-2051

POWER STUDIOS

Gigantic complex with performance spaces, art galleries, a bar, restaurant, and live music of diverse kinds nightly. In the unlikely event that nothing else appeals, venture up to the rooftop and gaze across the city. ✚ F3 ✉ 3701 N.E. 2nd Avenue ☎ 305/573-8042 🚌 9, 10

SANDBAR

Low-key bar and eatery with live, mostly local, rock music. ✚ Off map ✉ 3420 Main Highway, Coconut Grove ☎ 305/444-5270 🚇 Coconut Grove 🚌 42, 48

SUNDAY'S ON THE BAY

You need not partake of the pricey brunch in order to enjoy the live reggae performed every Sunday at the bar of this restaurant overlooking Biscayne Bay. Reggae and rock acts can also be found here on some weeknights. ✚ Off map ✉ 5420 Crandon Boulevard, Key Biscayne ☎ 305/361-6777 🚌 B

SUNRISE MUSICAL THEATER

A major venue for internationally known bands; concerts by major artists sell out months in advance. In northwest Miami; take a cab. ✚ Off map ✉ 5555 N.W. 95th Avenue ☎ 954/741-7300

TAURUS CHOPS

Fairly mellow neighborhood restaurant and general purpose hangout, with easy-going rock and R&B acts most nights. ✚ Off map ✉ 3540 Main Highway, Coconut Grove ☎ 305/443-5553 🚇 Coconut Grove 🚌 42, 48

TOBACCO ROAD

Having served its first drink in 1912 (it is the proud owner of Miami's liquor license No. 0001), Tobacco Road is Miami's oldest bar and unrivaled as its most atmospheric setting for top-notch blues and jazz artists. ✚ F8 ✉ 626 S. Miami Avenue ☎ 305/374-1198 🚇 Fifth Street 🚌 6, 8, 24, 48, 95, B

VAN DYKE CAFÉ

In an upstairs room of this busy café, the cream of local jazz musicians demonstrate their skills to an appreciative crowd. ✚ L6 ✉ 846 Lincoln Road ☎ 305/534-3600 🚌 K, F/M, S, W

Music in the open air

Barely a month passes without some kind of open-air concert in Miami. Major events include the Miami Reggae Festival (August at Bayfront Park) and the music-dominated Carnaval Miami, also known as Calle Ocho Festival (March in Little Havana). Or catch June's Goombay Festival in Coconut Grove's Peacock Park, Bayfront Park's Brazilian Festival in September and, at the same venue, November's Puerto Rican Festival.

NIGHTCLUBS

South Beach clubbing

Admission to South Beach nightclubs is often restricted to the kind of people the club owners want to see inside. If a club is popular among celebrities, door managers admit only the famous, fashionable, or glamorously attired. Most, however, admit anybody dressed with sensitivity to the style of the club. Expect long lines on Friday and Saturday nights. Cover charges of up to $10 are often waived before 9PM.

BASH

Draws celebrities to its bar, garden, and dance floor; spins everything from retro to house depending on the night's theme.
➕ M7 ✉ 655 Washington Avenue ☎ 305/538-2274
🚌 C, H, K, W

BERMUDA BAR & GRILL

An expansive disco well north of Downtown. From Top 40 to salsa, the musical fare varies; nightly special events can include free beer and bikini contests. Take a cab.
➕ Off map ✉ 3509 N.E. 163rd Street, north of Downtown ☎ 305/945-0196

CACTUS

Drag nights, pool competitions, and cut-price drink specials feature on various nights at this enormous gay complex.
➕ F7 ✉ 2041 Biscayne Boulevard ☎ 305/438-0662
🚌 3, 16

CLUB TROPIGALA

Stuck in a time warp but keeping its ostrich-plumed head held high, the Tropigala invites you to dine while watching a choreographed Vegas-cum pre-Revolutionary Havana-style show amid a profusion of foliage.
➕ N3 ✉ Foutainebleau Hilton, 4441 Collins Avenue ☎ 305/672-7469 🚌 C, F/M, G, H, L, S

CROBAR

Hottest nightspot on South Beach usually pulsating with techno and house plus a cast of larger-than-life regulars. Sunday is gay and lesbian night.
➕ M6 ✉ 1445 Washington Avenue ☎ 305/531-5027
🚌 C, H, K, W

GROOVE JET

A fashionable spot where you can watch South Beach's hipsters shaking a leg but still looking cool.
➕ M5 ✉ 323 23rd Street ☎ 305/532-2002 🚌 C, F/M, G, H, L, S

LEVEL

Multi-level nightspot on South Beach with four dance floors, three separate rooms, diverse sounds, and a fashionable but not ultra-cool crowd.
➕ M6 ✉ 1235 Washington Avenue ☎ 305/532-1525
🚌 C, H, K, W

LIQUID

Hip nightspot with two dance floors and theme nights. Sounds range from acid jazz and deep house to hip-hop and industrial.
➕ M6 ✉ 1439 Washington Avenue ☎ 305/532-9154
🚌 C, H, K, W

TWIST

Six venues in one with music and mood varying according to the night. Round-the-clock clubbers can arrive early for happy-hour, from 1PM to 9PM.
➕ M6 ✉ 1057 Washington Avenue ☎ 305/53-TWIST
🚌 C, H, K, W

WARSAW BALLROOM

An old-timer by Miami Beach standards; theme nights, top dance music, and a crowd of regulars.
➕ Off map ✉ 1450 Collins Avenue ☎ 305/531-4555
🚌 E, K, S, V

BARS

ABBEY BREWING COMPANY

A delightful bar with a good list of its own-brewed ales and other microbrews.

L6 ⊠ 1115 16th Street ☎ 305/538-8110 🚌 F/M, K, S

CLUB DEUCE

This unassuming but long-popular locals' bar—complete with pool players and bikers—is a no-frills joint that makes a great start, or end, to a fun South Beach night out.

M6 ⊠ 222 14th Street ☎ 305/673-9537 🚌 C, H, K, W

FAT TUESDAY

Frozen daiquiris, happy hours, and other cut-price deals. Part of the chain.

Off map ⊠ CocoWalk, 3015 Grand Avenue, Coconut Grove ☎ 305/441-2992 🚊 Coconut Grove 🚌 42, 48

GORDON BIERSCH BREWERY RESTAURANT

Workers in suits come from the adjacent banking district to sample the fine selection of microbrews and the food that complements them—be sure to try the garlic fries.

F9 ⊠ 1201 Brickell Avenue ☎ 786/425-1130 🚌 24, 48, J

JOHNMARTIN'S PUB

The sideroom of an Irish restaurant serves stouts and ales across a handsome mahogany bar.

Off map ⊠ 253 Miracle Mile, Coral Gables ☎ 305/445-3777 🚌 24, 40, 56, J

LOST WEEKENDS

A low-key local favorite, with a convivial crowd whiling the night away into the small hours.

M6 ⊠ 218 Española Way ☎ 305/672-1707 🚌 C, H, K, W

NORMAN'S TAVERN

Far enough north from lively SoBe to be relaxed, this hangout is a great place to eat and drink while watching the world go by on busy Collins Avenue.

Off map ⊠ 6770 Collins Avenue ☎ 305/868-9248 🚌 E, K, S, V

ROSEBAR

Splash out on a cocktail and paticipate in some superb people-watching at the ultra-chic lobby bar of the Delano Hotel (▶ 84). You can slink into a designer sofa or wander out to the beach deck.

M6 ⊠ 1685 Collins Avenue ☎ 305/672-2000 or 800/555-5001 🚌 C, G, F/M, H, L, S

TITANIC BREWERY & LOUNGE

Live blues and jazz, and lots of microbrews, some made on the premises.

Off map ⊠ 5813 Ponce De Leon Boulevard ☎ 305/667-ALES 🚌 24, 48

ZEKE'S ROADHOUSE

Microbrews from around the world make this a popular early-evening stop for SoBe clubbers.

M6 ⊠ 620 Lincoln Road ☎ 305/532-0081 🚌 K, F/M, S, W

Prohibition in Miami

Miami's reputation as a place to party is well-deserved. The city survived even Prohibition with comparative ease. The indented coastline made the landing of smuggled liquor from the Bahamas easy, while ineffective law enforcement coupled with the city's determination to give tourists what they wanted saw hotels and bars serving alcohol—from beer to top-class champagne—throughout the Prohibition period.

LUXURY HOTELS

Prices and discounts

The following rates are based on two people sharing a hotel's lowest-priced room (less tax) on a week night in low season (May–Sep); expect to pay 10–30 percent more in high season:

Luxury	over $200
Mid-Range	$100–$200
Budget	under $100
Hostel	$12–$14 per person

THE BILTMORE
The 280 rooms offer sumptuous elegance; a hotel with a special place in Miami's history (► 26).
➕ Off map ✉ 1200 Anastasia Avenue, Coral Gables ☎ 305/445-1926 or 800/727-1926; fax 305/913-280 🚍 24, 42, 72

THE DELANO
Miami's most fashionable hotel, with all-white interiors by Philippe Starck and a celebrity clientele.
➕ M6 ✉ 1685 Collins Avenue ☎ 305/672-2000 or 800/555-5001; fax 305/532-0099 🍽 C, G, F/M, H, L, S

THE FONTAINEBLEAU HILTON RESORT
Most of the 1,206 guest rooms, though comfortable, are less impressive than the design and spacious grounds of this landmark building (► 48).
➕ N3 ✉ 4441 Collins Avenue ☎ 305/538-2000 or 800/548-8886; fax 305/673-5351 🍽 C, F/M, G, H, L, S

GRAND BAY HOTEL
A sumptuous classic dripping with chandeliers, designer furnishings, and antiques. Popular with a star-studded clientele who want to relax away from SoBe and enjoy the views over Biscayne Bay.
➕ F9 ✉ 2669 S. Bayshore Drive, Coconut Grove ☎ 305/858-9600 or 800/327-2788; fax 305/859-2026 🚍 Coconut Grove 🚍 42, 48

LOEWS MIAMI BEACH
This giant hotel reaches SoBe with sumptuously landscaped grounds, straircases decorated with palm trees, and 800 luxurious rooms (and butler-staffed ocean-front cabanas).
➕ M6 ✉ 1601 Collins Avenue ☎ 305/604-1601 or 800/23-LOEWS; fax 305/604-1601 🍽 C, G, H, K, M, S, W

THE MARLIN
This gorgeous art-deco renovation draws many music stars, not least for the fully equipped recording studio.
➕ M7 ✉ 1200 Collins Avenue ☎ 305/604-5000 or 800/OUTPOST; fax 305/604-5000 🍽 C, H, K, W

PELICAN
Although you can stay here for less, the money-no-object guest can spend up to $2,000 a night on one of the 30 themed rooms that range from the cross-filled Jesus Christ Megastar to the fish-themed Some Like It Wet.
➕ M7 ✉ 826 Ocean Drive ☎ 305/673-3373 or 800/7-PELICAN; fax 305/673-3373 🍽 C, H, K, W

THE RALEIGH
A renovated 1940s landmark with 107 rooms, every conceivable facility, and a guest list of glitterati.
➕ M5 ✉ 1775 Collins Avenue ☎ 305/534-6300 or 800/848-1775; fax 305/538-8140 🍽 C, F/M, G, H, L, S

SONESTA BEACH RESORT
A relaxing 300-room beachside high-rise on peaceful Key Biscayne.
➕ Off map ✉ 350 Ocean Drive, Key Biscayne ☎ 305/361-2021 or 800/SONESTA; fax 305/365-2082 🍽 B

MID-RANGE HOTELS

THE COLONY
Much photographed for its stunning geometric design; small and friendly with just 50 rooms. A perfect South Beach base.

➕ M7 ✉ 736 Ocean Drive ☎ 305/673-0088 or 800/226-5669; fax 305/532-0762 🚌 C, H, K, W

DAVID WILLIAM
The 104 rooms are spacious and comfortable—the ideal Coral Gables location.

➕ Off map ✉ 700 Biltmore Way, Coral Gables ☎ 305/445-7821 or 800/327-8770; fax 305/913-1933 🚌 24, 40, 56, J

DOUBLETREE
Modern high-rise in the heart of Coconut Grove. Some of the 192 rooms have fantastic bay views.

➕ Off map ✉ 2649 S. Bayshore Drive, Coconut Grove ☎ 305/858-2500 or 800/222-8733; fax 305/858-9117 Ⓜ Coconut Grove 🚌 42, 48

HAMPTON INN
Generic but comfortable chain hotel, this is reasonably well located for exploring the city provided you have a car.

➕ Off map ✉ 2800 S.W. 28th Terrace, Coral Gables ☎ 305/448-2800; fax 305/442-8655 🚌 40, 56, J

INDIAN CREEK HOTEL
Inviting, restored art-deco hostelry with 61 rooms on a quiet street a short walk from the heart of South Beach. Geniune deco furnishings and a fine restaurant with some outdoor seating add to the charm.

➕ N4 ✉ 2727 Indian Creek Drive ☎ 305/531-2727 or 800/491-2772; fax 305/531-5651 🚌 C, F/M, G, H, L, S

PARK CENTRAL HOTEL
Art-deco hotel appealingly restored in 1940s style, with 128 cozy rooms and fine views that extend from Lummus Park to the ocean.

➕ M7 ✉ 640 Ocean Drive ☎ 305/538-1611 or 800/727-5236; fax 305/534-7520 🚌 C, H, K, W

PLACE ST. MICHEL
Art nouveau finds a Miami showcase in this renovated 1926 hotel with 27 individually furnished rooms and a warm, romantic atmosphere. Highly regarded restaurant.

➕ Off map ✉ 162 Alcazar Avenue, Coral Gables ☎ 305/444-1666 or 800/848-HOTEL; fax 305/528-0074 🚌 24, 40, 56, J

WALDORF TOWERS
An art-deco landmark in the heart of SoBe with 45 compact and functional rooms. Those at the front have ocean views.

➕ M7 ✉ 860 Ocean Drive ☎ 305/531-7684 or 800/933-BEACH; fax 305/672-6836 🚌 C, H, K, W

THE WAVE
South Beach is spreading south of 5th Street, and this 65-room hotel is among the first to offer accommodations with style in this up-and-coming area. Price includes continental breakfast.

➕ M7 ✉ 350 Ocean Drive ☎ 305/673-0401 or 800/501-0401; fax 305/531-9385 🚌 H, K

Longer stays

Apartments can be much better value than hotels for a longer than average stay in Miami. Though many require a six-month minimum rental, some apartments are available by the month. In South Beach, prices are typically around $500 a month for a studio; $600–$700 for a 1-bedroom apartment; $700–$1000 for two bedrooms. Renter's Connection (☎ 800/439-9203) is a no-fee apartment rental agency.

BUDGET ACCOMMODATIONS

Reservation services

The following companies provide information on Miami accommodations and can make reservations on your behalf: Budget Reservations Service (✉ 1437 Collins Avenue, Miami Beach, FL 33139 ☎ 305/532-7273 or 800/681-1993); Central Reservation Service (☎ 9010 S.W. 137th Avenue, Suite 116, Miami, FL 33186 ☎ 800/950-0232); Florida Sunbreak (✉ 169 Lincoln Road, Miami Beach, FL 33139 ☎ 305/532-1516 or 888-SUNBREAK); and South Florida Hotel Network (✉ 300 71st Street, Miami Beach, FL 33141 ☎ 305/538-3616; 800/538-3616).

THE ABBEY
A ten-minute walk to the beach and a slightly longer one to the heart of trendy South Beach means this well-presented art-deco hotel can offer some of the neighborhood's best rates. Restaurant and roof-top bar.
✚ M5 ✉ 300 21st Street ☎ 305/531-0031 or 888/612-2239; fax 305/672-1663 🖃 All serving South Beach

AVALON & MAJESTIC
Restored art-deco hotel in the heart of South Beach with 108 unelaborate but comfortable rooms. Fun bar and a good long-standing restaurant.
✚ M7 ✉ 700 Ocean Drive ☎ 305/538-0133 or 800/933-3306; fax 305/534-0258 🖃 C, H, K, W

BANANA BUNGALOW
Low-cost dormitory with slightly pricier private rooms, a block from the ocean and a few minutes' walk from South Beach.
✚ M5 ✉ 2360 Collins Avenue ☎ 305/538-1173 or 800/7HOSTEL; fax 305/531-3217 🖃 C, F/M, H, L, S

BAYLISS GUESTHOUSE
Modest South Beach base offering a choice of 21 spick-and-span rooms. Located on a quiet side-street that erupts with children when classes let out at the school across the street. Gay friendly.
✚ M6 ✉ 504 14th Street ☎ 305/531-3755 or 800/305-4683; fax 305/532-3755 🖃 C, H, K, W

BRIGHAM GARDENS
Tropical birds and vegetation fill the grounds of this small and friendly spot with 19 rooms and suites.
✚ M6 ✉ 1411 Collins Avenue ☎ 305/531-1331; fax 305/538-9898 🖃 C, H, K, W

THE CLAY HOTEL & INTERNATIONAL HOSTEL
Simple private rooms and small dormitories in a 1920s Mediterranean-style building.
✚ M6 ✉ 1438 Washington Avenue ☎ 305/534-2988 or 800/379-CLAY; fax 305/673-0346 🖃 C, H, K, W

ESSEX HOUSE
A 1930s Moderne hotel tastefully restored; with 79 relaxing rooms. Café.
✚ M7 ✉ 1001 Collins Avenue ☎ 305/534-2700 or 800/553-7739; fax 305/532-3827 🖃 C, H, K, W

MIAMI BEACH INTERNATIONAL TRAVELLERS HOSTEL
Low-priced shared dormitories and inexpensive private rooms; well located with a spacious kitchen.
✚ M7 ✉ 236 9th Street ☎ 305/534-0268; fax 305/534-5862 🖃 C, H, K, W

RIVIERA COURT
Simple motel with 30 rooms in a quiet setting near the University of Miami, a useful base if you have a car.
✚ Off map ✉ 5100 Riviera Drive, Coral Gables ☎ 305/665-3528 or 800/368-8602; fax 305/667-8993 🖃 42, J

MIAMI
travel facts

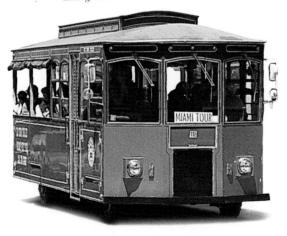

Planning Your Trip

When to go

- October to March are Miami's busiest months, sunny and warm with comfortable humidity.
- Peak periods are over Christmas and New Year.
- To avoid crowds and the highest prices, visit in April or September, though be prepared for humid weather.
- Events and festivals take place throughout the year.

Climate

- Warm and sunny year-round with little variation in temperature, Miami experiences its highest humidity during the summer months.
- Humidity drops through the fall; winter is pleasant.
- Summer is marked by short, sharp thunderstorms.
- Hurricane season is from June to November. The tropical depressions that can grow into hurricanes as they cross the Caribbean are carefully tracked by radar. Miami receives at least several days' warning of potential hurricanes; most either dissipate or bypass the city.
- Air-conditioning is ubiquitous and often set very cold; bring a sweater.

Arriving & Departing

Arriving by air

- Miami International Airport, 7 miles west of downtown and 14 miles west of Miami Beach, handles all international and virtually all domestic flights into the city.
- Super Shuttle ☎ 305/871-2000 run minibuses between the airport and the city. Fares are calculated according to the postal zip code of your destination and are prominently displayed on noticeboards (as are those of taxis) outside the baggage claim area. Passengers collect a shuttle boarding pass from the ticket stand and pay the driver on arrival. The trip to Miami Beach usually takes around 30 minutes depending on the number of people to be dropped off.
- City buses also serve the airport, departing from the Metrobus stop outside Concourse E. The "J" serves Miami Beach (taking 40 minutes to reach 41st Street) and, in other directions, Coral Gables (15 minutes) and Coconut Grove (30 minutes). Bus 7 links the airport with downtown (30 minutes); bus 37 with Coconut Grove (30 minutes).
- Taxis serve all parts of the city from the airport; flat fare to Miami Beach is $22 for the approximately 25-minute ride.
- Airport information ☎ 305/876-7000

Arriving by bus

- All Greyhound buses into Miami arrive at the Miami Bayside terminal, downtown ✉ 700 Biscayne Boulevard. Some also serve the airport Greyhound terminal ✉ 4111 N.W. 27th Street
- Information ☎ 800/231-2222

Arriving by car

- I–90 is one of the main routes from the north, but be warned that this highway is undergoing extensive construction and the road works will cause delays. The alternative is Florida's Turnpike, which is a toll road (☎ 800/749–7453 for details of tolls and other services). If you are coming from the northwest use I–75 or US–27; from the south US–1 or the Homestead Extension of Florida's Turnpike are the best routes; from the west use I–75 or US–41.

- Improvements to highways within the Greater Miami area, including the Golden Glades interchange, widening of the MacArthur Causeway, and the new Brickell Avenue Bridge, are now making driving easier.

Arriving by train

- Amtrak trains terminate at 8303 N.W. 37th Avenue, 7 miles north-west of Downtown.
- The Amtrak station is served by bus L, which runs to Miami Beach, and is close to a Metrorail terminal that provides access to Downtown.
- Information ☎ 800/872-7245

Departure and airport tax

- These are included in the cost of your plane ticket.

ESSENTIAL FACTS

Usual opening hours

- Shops: Mon–Sat 9 or 10–5 or 6. Department stores, supermarkets, and malls keep longer hours, as do many of the shops in Miami Beach.
- Sunday shopping is common.
- Bank hours: Mon to Fri 9 to 3, with many branches open later once or more a week.

National holidays

- New Year's Day (Jan 1)
- Martin Luther King Day (third Mon in Jan)
- President's Day (third Mon in Feb)
- Memorial Day (last Mon in May)
- Independence Day (July 4)
- Labor Day (first Mon in Sep)
- Columbus Day (second Mon in Oct); affecting only banks and federal offices
- Veteran's Day (Nov 11)
- Thanksgiving Day (fourth Thu in Nov)
- Christmas Day (Dec 25)

Money matters

- Most banks have automatic teller machines (ATMs).
- Credit cards are widely accepted in stores and restaurants.
- A 6.5 percent sales tax is added to marked retail prices; additional taxes (of 3–6 percent) apply to hotel accommodations and to meals in some restaurants (making total taxes of 10.5–12.5 percent).

Etiquette

- Smoking is banned in many public buildings and on public transportation. Smokers intending to light up in a restaurant should ensure they are in the designated "smoking section."

Tipping

- Tip at least 15 percent of the bill in a restaurant; 15 percent of the taxi fare; and $1 per bag for a hotel porter.

Travelers with disabilities

- Numerous organizations can provide information and services to visitors with disabilities. A good place to start is the Miami-Dade Office of ADA Co-ordination ✉ 111 N.W. 1st Street, 12th floor, Suite 348 ☎ 305/375-3566

Tourist information

Visitor Information Centers:

- Art Deco Welcome Center ✉ 1001 Ocean Drive, Miami Beach ☎ 305/672-2014
- Miami Beach Chamber of

Commerce ✉ 420 Lincoln Road, Miami Beach ☎ 305/672-1210
- Coconut Grove Chamber of Commerce ✉ 2820 McFarlane Road, Coconut Grove ☎ 305/444-7270
- Tropical Everglades Visitor Association ✉ 160 Highway 1, Florida City ☎ 800/388-9669
- Greater Miami Convention & Visitors Bureau ✉ 701 Brickell Avenue, Downtown ☎ 800/283-2707

Student travelers
- Travelers carrying an International Student Identity Card (ISIC) can get reduced admission to many attractions.

Time differences
- Miami is on Eastern Standard Time, three hours ahead of the West Coast, five hours behind the U.K., six hours behind Western Europe, and 13–15 hours behind Australia.

PUBLIC TRANSPORTATION

- Travel between neighborhoods is relatively easy with the public transportation network of buses and the elevated single-route railway, Metrorail.
- In and immediately around Downtown, the Metromover monorail provides efficient if slow movement.
- Services become sporadic after the evening rush hour.
- Don't use public transportation at night especially away from Miami Beach.
- Transit information ☎ 305/770-3131

Buses
- Fare, $1.25; transfer to different bus route or Metrorail within two hours, 25c.

- Exact fare only, using bills, coins, and/or tokens.
- To transfer to Metrorail ask for "rail transfer."
- To transfer to Metromover ask for "Metromover transfer" (free).
- Fare tokens cost $10 for a set of 10 and can also be used on Metrorail.

Metromover
- Fare, 25c. Pay in exact change at turnstile.
- To transfer to bus, push "Metrobus transfer" button on turnstile. Give the issued transfer, plus $1, to bus driver.
- To transfer to Metrorail, insert $1 into Metrorail turnstile.

Metrorail
- Fare, $1.25; 25c to transfer to bus.
- Buy a bus transfer from the machine inside the station as you enter.
- A morning transfer can be used until noon; an afternoon transfer from noon until midnight.
- Fare tokens cost $10 for 10 and can be used on buses.

Tokens and change
- Tokens can be purchased from Metrorail stations, from the Transit Information centers on level two of Government Center Station, at the Omni Station, and at the Transit Information Center at the corner of Flagler Street and S.E. 1st Avenue, Downtown.
- Change machines are found at Metrorail stations.

Schedules and map information
- Maps showing public transportation routes and individual bus and Metrorail schedules, are available from the Transit Information centers listed above; each bus usually

carries schedules for the route it serves and useful adjoining routes.

Taxis

- Can be hailed on the street, and are found outside major hotels, at airports, and, bus and train stations. It is more common, however, to telephone for one.
- Hotel receptionists, restaurant staff, and nightclub staff will usually be happy to order a taxi on request.
- During rush hours and rain showers, taxis are in heavy demand.
- Fares are $1.75 per mile. Miami taxi drivers undergo courtesy training as a condition of acquiring a license.
- Should you have any complaints about them ☎ 305/375-2460
- Miami taxi firms include:
  Flamingo ☎ 305/759-8100
  Metro ☎ 305/888-8888
  Yellow ☎ 305/444-4444

DRIVING

Car rental

- There is enormous choice of car rental companies in the Greater Miami area. Rates for rental range from $26 a day or $155 a week, exclusive of the 6.5 percent tax.
- Discounts on car rental may be available to senior citizens, members of auto clubs, and members of Hostelling International—American Youth Hostels.
- Promotional discounts can be even more generous, so check what is on offer when making your reservation.
- Rental companies include:
  Alamo ☎ 800/327-9633
  Avis ☎ 800/331-1600
  Budget ☎ 800/527-0700
  Dollar ☎ 800/800-4000
  Hertz ☎ 800/654-3131

National InterRent ☎ 800/227-7368
Value ☎ 800/468-2583

- In comparing prices, ask about drop-off charges and one-way service fees, which can be hefty.
- Check the coverage provided by your personal auto insurance policy before you rent a car. If it is not adequate, or if you do not have personal auto insurance, you can obtain protection from the rental company that will cover damage to the car for the duration of the rental. Known as loss-damage waiver (LDW), or collision-damage waiver (CDW), this coverage is optional and costs in the region of $14 a day.
- If you are traveling with babies or young children, you can arrange to rent car seats (which are compulsory for all children under the age of five). Be sure to book them in advance when you reserve your car.

Driving regulations

- Florida has very tough laws against drink driving. The maximum level is so low, it is best not to drink alcolhol at all when driving.
- Florida speed limits: 55–70 miles per hour on highways; 20–30 miles per hour in residential areas and 15 miles per hour near schools. Highway Patrol strongly enforce these limits including minimum speeds on some interstates, which require motorists to drive at over 40 miles per hour.

MEDIA AND COMMUNICATIONS

Telephones

- Local calls usually cost 35c for the first 15 minutes.
- Calls made from hotel-room telephones are usually more

expensive than calls made on a
public telephone.

Post offices

- Main post office ✉ 2200 Milam Dairy
Road ☎ 305/639-4280. Letters marked
"General Delivery" can be col-
lected by their intended recipient
(with suitable identification) from
the Downtown post office
✉ 500 N.W. 2nd Avenue
- For general postal queries
☎ 305/470-8222

Newspapers

- The city's major daily newspaper
is the *Miami Herald*. Best of
several free weeklies is *New Times*,
with local news and features, and
entertainment and restaurant
listings.

Magazines

- Glossy monthly magazines such
as *South Florida* reflect the glamorous side of Miami living. The
free *TWN* is the main weekly gay
and lesbian newspaper. Free
tourist magazines include *Welcome*
and several publications of the
Convention and Visitors Bureau,
including *Tropical Miami* and
Cultural Guide.

Radio

- The AM waveband is generally
best for news and talk, and
includes the all-news station
WINZ (940AM). The FM waveband has a wide variety of music
stations. The National Public
Radio station, WLRN (91.3FM),
usually carries the best current
affairs features.

Television

- The main Miami TV channels are
4 WCIX (CBS), 6 WTVJ (NBC),
7 WSVN (FOX), 10 WPLG
(ABC), 17 WLRN (PBS), 23

WLTV (independent), 33 WBFS
(independent).
- Most hotels offer several cable
TV channels and pay-per-view
movies.

International newsagents

- A number of newsstands stock
overseas newspapers and magazines, including the News Café
✉ 800 Ocean Drive, Miami Beach, and
Barnes & Noble ✉ 152 Miracle Mile,
Coral Gables

EMERGENCIES

Sensible precautions

- Always be vigilant. Watch out for
the "sunshine" signs, which direct
you towards main tourist areas.
- By day, all major areas of interest
to visitors are relatively safe but
after dark stick to established
nightlife areas and never take
short cuts through dark alleys.
Neighborhoods can change from
safe to dangerous within a few
blocks.
- Before using public transportation, discuss your itinerary with
your hotel reception staff and
heed their advice.
- Women and lone travelers are not
unusual in Miami and women in
particular may encounter
unwanted attention after dark.
Avoid being alone on the street
outside established nightlife
spots. If you are waiting for a cab,
do so inside the club or restaurant,
or at least somewhere where staff
can see you.
- Never carry easily snatched bags
and cameras, and don't place your
wallet into your back pocket. In a
bar or restaurant, make sure you
keep your belongings within sight
and within reach. Women should
never let a shoulder bag dangle

on the back of their chair in a restaurant.

- Leave cameras and other valuables in your hotel's safe when you're not using them. Never carry more money than you need. Pay for major purchases with traveler's checks or credit cards.
- Read and heed the instructions when you buy traveler's checks and carry the instructions with you—separate from the checks.
- If only in order to make your insurance claim, you should report any item that has been stolen to the nearest police precinct.

Lost property
- Miami International Airport ☎ 305/876-7377
- Lost on Metro–Dade transit ☎ 305/595-6263
- Police Lost & Found ☎ 305/375-3366

Medical treatment
- Ask your hotel reception staff for referrals or phone the non-emergency Physician Referral Service 🕐 Mon–Fri 9–5 ☎ 305/324-8717, or the Emergency Dental Referral Service ☎ 305/285-5470
- In an emergency go to a hospital with a 24-hour emergency room, such as Health South Doctor's Hospital ✉ 5000 University Drive, Coral Gables ☎ 305/666-2111

Medicines
- If you are using medication regularly, bring a supply with you.
- There are plenty of late night pharmacies all over the city, and the following are open around-the-clock:
  Eckerd ✉ 1825 Miami Gardens Drive ☎ 305/932-5740
  Walgreen's ✉ 5731 Bird Road ☎ 305/666-0757

Emergency telephone numbers
- Fire, police, or ambulance ☎ 911 (no money required).
- Attorney ☎ 305/931-0100
- Rape Hotline ☎ 305/585-7273 (to report a rape); ☎ 305/585-6949 (for recovery support).

Consulates
- Canada
  ✉ 200 S. Biscayne Boulevard
  ☎ 305/579-1600
- Germany
  ✉ 100 N. Biscayne Boulevard
  ☎ 305/358-0290
- Italy
  ✉ 1200 Brickell Avenue
  ☎ 305/374-6322
- Netherlands
  ✉ 801 Brickell Avenue
  ☎ 305/789-6646
- Norway
  ✉ 1001 North America Way
  ☎ 305/358-4386
- U.K.
  ✉ 1001 Brickell Bay Drive
  ☎ 305/374-1522

INDEX

Citypack
Miami

AUTHOR *Mick Sinclair*
COVER DESIGN *Tigist Getachew*
MANAGING EDITOR *Jackie Staddon*
COVER PICTURES *AA Photo Library*

Copyright	©Automobile Association Developments Limited 1997, 2001
Maps copyright	©Automobile Association Developments Limited 1997, 2001
Fold-out map	© RV Reise- und Verkehrsverlag Munich · Stuttgart
	© Cartography: GeoData

Published in the United Kingdom by AA Publishing

ISBN 0-676-90155-7
Second Edition

Acknowledgments

The Automobile Association wishes to thank the following photographers, libraries and associations for their assistance in the preparation of this book:
American Police Hall of Fame and Museum 41a; Collection Bass Museum of Art 47a (Peter Paul Rubens Studio), 47b (Gift of John and Joanna Bass); Stewart Bates 61a; Fairchild Tropical Garden 23b, 30; Fontainebleau Hilton 48; Greater Miami Convention and Visitors Bureau 57a; Historical Museum of Southern Florida 5a, 37; Erika Klass/Hillstrom Stock Photo, Inc. 34a; Lowe Art Museum, Florida 23a, 27a, 27b; Norman McGrath 39a, 39b; Pictures Colour Library 6/7, 15, 58; Rex Features Ltd 12 (C. Brown), 57b; Susan Russell/Hillstrom Stock Photo, Inc. 34b, 38; Sanford L. Ziff Jewish Museum of Florida 46; Spectrum Colour Library 17, 50/1, 53, 62b; The Wolfsonian Foundation 45b; Zefa Pictures Ltd 21, 25a, 60.
All remaining pictures were taken by Jon Davison and are held in the Association's own library (AA Photo Library) with the exception of the following pages: Pete Bennett 13b, 29, 54, 57b, 59, 61b; David Lyons 1, 6, 8, 32a, 32b, 40, 44, 45a; Lanny Provo 20, 31, 36b; Antony Souter 49b; Peter Timmermans 43b.

Important tip

Time inevitably brings changes, so always confirm prices, travel facts, and other perishable information when it matters. Although Fodor's cannot accept responsiblity for errors, you can use this guide in the confidence that we have taken every care to ensure its accuracy.

Special sales

Fodor's Travel Publications are available at special discounts for bulk purchases (100 copies or more) for sales promotions or premiums. Special editions, including personalized covers, excerpts of existing guides, and corporate imprints, can be created in large quantities for special needs. For more information, contact your local bookseller or write to Special Markets, Fodor's Travel Publications, 280 Park Avenue, New York NY 10017. Inquiries from Canada should be directed to your local Canadian bookseller or sent to Random House of Canada Ltd., Marketing Department, 2775 Matheson Blvd. East, Mississauga, Ontario L4W 4P7.

Color separation by Daylight Colour Art Pte Ltd, Singapore
Manufactured by Dai Nippon Printing Co. (Hong Kong) Ltd
10 9 8 7 6 5 4 3 2 1

Titles in the Citypack series

- Amsterdam • Barcelona • Beijing • Berlin • Boston • Brussels & Bruges •
- Chicago • Dublin • Florence • Hong Kong • Lisbon • London • Los Angeles •
- Madrid • Melbourne • Miami • Montreal • Munich • New York • Paris •
- Prague • Rome • San Francisco • Seattle • Shanghai • Singapore • Sydney •
- Tokyo • Toronto • Vienna • Venice • Washington, D.C. •